DARK SUN:

A NEW APPROACH TO FAMILIES AND ADDICTION

BY FRANCIS LICKERISH

COPYRIGHT

I would like to dedicate this book to the memory of George Aubrey Lyward OBE who consistently urged me to 'resist the strong pull of the herd'; to my Brother David who, probably unwittingly, saved my life; and to Ondine, everybody should have a daughter like you.

INTRODUCTION

'Every stick has two ends'

Mullah Nasruddin

I offer this book as a challenge – even as a confrontation. All authorities, the World Health Organisation included, agree that addiction is a family illness. When it arises in a family, it does so because conditions are favourable. Just as if addiction were a parasite or a virus, addiction cannot thrive where the culture is healthy and connected. The culture is, of course, the family, and not just the immediate here and now of Mum, Dad, Gran and little sister.

In these pages I shall write about the family in several respects. Every family has a provenance that extends back into the fogs of history – and forwards into a future stretching away into a blue yonder of lovely possibilities and expectations – to that wonderful condition known as Happy Ever After. This provenance and future have a powerful bearing on what is taking place today. The historical family and the future family must be understood as separate concepts which may exist within the same entity.

I will also write about the many different contexts in which addiction can manifest itself. In my experience, families have particular beliefs, principles, morals, worldviews, and religions. It is even true that families have what you might call systemic feelings. There are anxious families, angry families, happy families, and shame-based families. One may often come across military families, legal families, Christian families; families of every denomination. There are middle class, working class, upper class and classless families. I will show that in close-knit units like families it is therefore helpful when you come up against a particular quandary or habit of thought to ask yourself: "Whose thoughts am I thinking?"

This book is in part an exploration as to what all this might mean in relation to addiction. Where do these thought-paradigms originate? Whose idea were they? How did they come about and how deep do they run in our lives? How much of what I call "I" is made up of external archetypes? These inherited perspectives, those opinions and worldviews absorbed from the past – that is, from family, religious, political, social and cultural environments – might seem at first glance to be irrelevant. But they are not – and we only think them so because we are in a sort of fog and we don't know who we are.

In fact, in the context of the addicted family system these constructs which we have wrongly taken into ourselves are fundamental and significant. In this book, I will suggest that as a part of genuinely growing up we might begin to consider disentangling ourselves from our histories and perceived cultures as a route to true individuality. We shall investigate how much may be gained by whole-heartedly, and in an entirely new way, entering into recovery from the family illness of addiction. Perhaps it is difficult to see past the apparent obvious simplicity of family addiction the cruel yet seductive deceit that if the addict recovers and stops drinking, using or acting out all will be well and the system can return to a comfortable status quo.

I understand why we might want a return to that, but I shall show that as a notion it is dangerously cosy. Instead, I want to show that there is a different route – one which is more challenging, but ultimately more rewarding. The whole family – that means each individual member and the system as a whole – needs to engage, jointly and severally, in a recovery process that is separate from the recovery process of the identified addict. This means entering into some sort of growing up, some manner of therapeutic process.

In my experience, confronted with this reality, many people seek not to engage. "But I am alright, I don't need therapy!" the cry so often goes up, usually from people who don't actually know what therapy is or how it works and are, essentially, terrified of encountering themselves in a therapeutic relationship. That's fine, of course, and it's not altogether surprising that people can be anxious about making the sort of commitment which I am describing. Even so, I'm sorry to say that this strategy of avoidance amounts to a severe misconception. Those who have never had therapy simply don't know how much may be gained by that process. In reality, no matter how happy and self-reliant you think you are, there is a great deal you can do to fix yourself, to take responsibility for your part in whatever might be going wrong in your family, to begin to set boundaries and care for yourself. In short, it is possible to reclaim your life and all you might have lost from the terrifying despotic spectre of addiction.

There is a saying that recovery is the gift of addiction and this is very true. The personal demands made by the recovery process can and will, if engaged with, lead to a better quality of life no matter what the identified addict gets up to.

I am writing this book in the belief that there is always space for another perspective, especially in an area so murky and filled with apparent contradictions as this one. I don't intend this to be a learned book. Where it's "evidence-based", the evidence is entirely anecdotal and subjective, being drawn almost entirely from my own experience of 25 years working with groups and individuals enmeshed in the ghastly webs of addiction.

It is a book intended to be of use to people. I have included relevant case histories at the beginning of each chapter, and exercises which readers can undertake at the end. A great deal of literature, and indeed help, is there for the addicted soul but nowhere near so much is available to the family and such that does exist is, more often than not, covertly or overtly from the addict's point of view. This is something I wish to challenge from the outset. The family suffers as much – and often more – than the addict. This book is for those people, the ones left behind with little support, understanding or explanation.

F.L.
Gillingham, May 2024

CONTENTS

Dedication   *iii*

Introduction   *v*

CHAPTERS

PART ONE: INTO THE WILD

1   The Nature of Addiction   3

2   Addiction as a Spiritual Disease   23

3   What is a Family?   49

PART TWO: THE JOURNEY HOME

4   The Need for Change   75

5   What on Earth Can I Do Now?   91

6   Six Impossible Things Before Breakfast   109

7   Towards the Unexpected   119

Further Reading   *129*

Acknowledgements   *130*

Dark Sun:

A New Approach to Families and Addiction

PART ONE: INTO THE WILD

Dark Sun:

A New Approach to Families and Addiction

CHAPTER ONE

THE NATURE OF ADDICTION

Mulla Nasruddin went to the market and saw a big bushel of hot chilli peppers on sale. He bought them, returned home, and began to eat. A little while later, his disciples came and saw the Mulla with tears streaming down his face, his mouth and tongue burning. "Mulla, Mulla, why do you go on eating them?" As he reached for another, Nasruddin replied, "I keep waiting for a sweet one, and anyway, now I'm eating my money!"

Case History 1

A husband and wife came to see me. Their 25 year old son, let's call him Hugo, was in active addiction and, just like any other addiction victim, was causing mayhem and misery throughout the family system. The couple had two children, a son and a daughter. The daughter, being somewhat older, had left home and was living and working quite independently. The son, however, although no longer at home, was entirely dependent on his parents, having become enmeshed with narcotics of various kinds during his early teens.

The parents could not be certain as to the nature of his drug use; cannabis was certainly high profile as were cocaine and ketamine. He was also misusing his prescribed ADHD medication which he was obtaining from a private doctor for whom his parents were paying. They were also paying for his accommodation, buying his food and giving him an allowance. They were doing all this simply because they were afraid of doing otherwise. Shame, guilt, fear and anger kept them locked into maladaptive patterns of behaviour and had them trapped in a prison of anxiety. Hugo's addiction manipulated his parents and exercised powerful negative control over them using threats of suicide, further drug use and even violence. He volubly blamed his parents for his current situation, insisting that somehow, they owed him the level of support they were giving him and more. He repeatedly bullied (I use the word consciously) his mother into paying for his repeat private doctor appointments and repeat prescriptions. Hugo was remarkably adept at charming and convincing the doctor of his ADHD and need for continuing medication. The doctor knew nothing of Hugo's drug and alcohol use; Hugo made quite sure of that.

The family system found itself in a hostage situation from which there seemed no escape. His parents' lives were taken over by the addiction: it had, in fact, become the organising principle of the system and they could find no way out. All their other life roles as friends, employers and employees, husband and wife, parents to their daughter and all the other components of a once full and happy life had become subsumed in Hugo's addiction. It was in desperation that they came to me after what was to me a very familiar and sadly fruitless round of doctors, psychiatrists and therapists.

After listening to their story, I asked one or two questions. What are you hoping will happen? What is the evidence that this method will work? When will you know that you have had enough? Enquiries along these lines. As is so often the case in these situations, the parents' shame and guilt had them locked into this pattern. The only means at their disposal of alleviating the monstrous anxiety they were suffering was to continue along this path. I told them of the three Cs of family work:

You didn't cause it
You can't control it
You can't cure it.

At first they struggled with this new idea, but on being asked how well their guilt and shame had served them, they began to change their thinking just a little. I suggested that they begin to practise letting go. I stress the word practise because letting go is frightening and can be difficult. It involves something of what the Greeks would call a 'metanoia' – a change of mind.

I suggested that they stop paying for the doctor and the prescriptions; Hugo is an adult and can be responsible for himself. The mother became anxious at this, saying he would become abusive, threaten suicide and might even become violent. Once again reassuring her that none of this was her fault, I told her simply to let him get on with it and to do her best not to engage with the threats, even hang up the phone if necessary and if he appeared in person threatening violence, to call the police. Whenever I suggest calling the police, or the ambulance services or any other external resource that might intervene, it provides something of a shock and hints somewhat towards the potential seriousness of the situation.

Over time, the parents were increasingly able to put in boundaries that allowed them to give the problem back to Hugo and distance themselves, little by little, from his pathology. They also ceased to be a part of a covert support system, something that the addiction will always endeavour to set up.

This is a typical case where I see my task as holding up a mirror to the seriousness of the situation and providing tools whereby the family can begin to practise letting go and disentangle themselves from their loved ones' pathology.

THE SHAPE OF THE NIGHTMARE

So here you are. It is half past two in the morning. Sleep is impossible. Your metabolism is awash with cortisol, adrenaline and all sorts of other busy autonomic chemicals, all insisting that something quite ghastly has happened or is about to happen. You don't know how you got here: all you know is that somehow you went wrong. It might be something to do with the complex twists and turns which your life has taken – it's impossible to locate precisely how it all happened. In fact, the nature of the disaster which is about to happen is impossible to decipher, but the blame is easy to assign. It's because of *you*.

In fact, the feeling might be worse than this: it's because you didn't measure up. You haven't been good enough, and you certainly didn't do enough. You failed to come up with the right words at the right time, and the apposite actions. Nothing you did fit the situation, and so now you're in a busy little psychic hornet's nest, and you deserve to be there because it's all your own creation.

And you also know whose fault it isn't. It's not the fault of the person from whom the disaster, you know, is emanating. It's not because of your husband, wife, son, daughter, or friend who, let's say, 'just popped out' six hours ago and hasn't called since. Their phone goes straight to answering machine and that fact alone conjures up a whole range of images too horrible to contemplate, but which you have no choice but to enlarge on while you wait to hear the precise nature of what has happened. Your head and heart are full of perhapses. But there's one perhaps you won't entertain: that perhaps this isn't your fault after all.

The comforting rationalisations and excuses no longer work or are no longer appropriate. *The traffic on the High Street must have been dreadful. I expect the supermarket has sold out of….. and they've had to go further afield.* These justifications are losing their force – in fact they long since lost their ability to explain away this sort of situation. So what are you left with? An agony of anxiety, anger, and shame. Perhaps there was a row of some sort, or you weren't understanding or patient or kind or attractive enough. There is deep down in the very profundities of your being this nagging sense that somehow this is your fault.

It's not your fault. The truth is the person you care about is an addict. You are not. You just care about that person.

THE ADDICT'S PERSPECTIVE

So how does this all look from the addict's side of things? It looks very different, I can assure you. Perhaps they are on an impromptu alcohol or cocaine binge, cosied up in some sort of Spearmint Rhino, their evening about to take shape. They might be at a casino, betting the cost of your mortgage – and look here is the roulette ball refusing to land on the number they'd chosen. Maybe they're feeling ambitious, and they're on a 747, bound for Bali, striking out for the next chapter in their addiction. Most of the time, the truth is more prosaic: they're slumped at a bus stop, mouth lolling, asleep on the roadside, unnoticed and uncared-for.

Whatever they're up to, one thing seems likely: they're not thinking about the effect of all this on you, the worrier in their life. Addiction, I'm afraid, is an entirely self-centred condition.

Let's take an example – because the specifics of the situation are what makes it so awful. The kinds of crises I am describing are never appalling in theory – they are appalling in reality, and reality is always detailed, and horribly so when you are in the midst of crisis. Perhaps you are an adult daughter and your alcoholic mother is leaning on you for emotional support. Your mother will not acknowledge that she has a problem. She is constantly putting herself in dangerous situations, having blackouts during which she might lose a tooth or even break an arm without remembering what had happened. She is forever threatening to end her life. If challenged over her behaviour, she becomes angry and abusive. Her addiction has taken her daughter hostage, and the daughter feels responsible for her mother's safety and well-being to the extent that she cannot help but blame herself.

In years of practice, I have come to realise this hard truth: at no time does it occur to the addict that their behaviour is causing great pain to other people. They simply are not able to care. The addicted mind is deeply fearful and therefore unable to love anything other than itself and sadly the addict loves their drink, or their drug or their cherished behaviour patterns much more than they love you. It follows that the addicted mind is contemptuous, arrogant and highly manipulative. It will lie, deny, threaten, cajole and gaslight to get what it wants and to avoid being challenged or confronted. The tragedy in all this is that the addict truly believes they are right, that you cannot possibly understand what is going on and their drinking or drug use is perfectly reasonable and necessary: like a vampire, the addict fears the light of truth and cannot see their reflection in any mirror.

The fact that an addict can strongly believe their own illusions makes them potent and convincing liars and manipulators because they believe absolutely that what they are telling you is the truth. There is also a powerful investment in being misunderstood, since being misunderstood gives the addict permission to continue. As a family member, you will be told that you can't possibly understand the subtlety and depth of the addict's suffering and any attempts at trying to do so will be met with contempt. The family member needs to keep at the forefront of their mind that they are no longer dealing with the person they love. Instead, they are being used by an addicted entity that cares for nothing except protecting its own delusional self-image and its own gratification. Does this sound harsh? Perhaps it is good if it does, since the reality is harsh indeed.

THE PHENOMENON OF DENIAL

Denial is a curious phenomenon – and it is this symptom which makes the illness of addiction so difficult to treat. It is the only disease that tells you you haven't got it. It is full of distortions and false tracks: it is a terrible treachery visited on the self by itself, whereby the patient has a secret longing to get worse. If it were not for denial, it would be a simple matter to treat this horrible condition. The sufferer would just have to stop drinking, using and acting out. They would then have to follow and internalise some new and enlivening principles and all would be well. In such a world, the solution would be linear and logical; it would be eminently achievable.

Sadly, this is not the case in the crucial realm of reality. In truth, every addict will suffer denial, and almost always this denialism will spread into the ecosystem of the broader family. Denial is the mechanism by which the pathology spreads and creeps like a cancer into the family system. Since it tends to impinge into the fabric of each family where addiction occurs, it also has a bewildering array of manifestations. Sometimes these can be very ridiculous – the slurringly drunken denial that the addict has been drinking before they pass out on the stairs for the night.

That might seem absurd, and perhaps even addiction can have its comic or farcical aspects, but there are other more subtle and invidious ways in which denial can present.

"Have you taken something? It's just that you don't seem quite…"

"No of course I haven't darling, I'm just tired. Don't you think you are being just a little bit controlling. I know you think I'm a problem, but perhaps the problem is…. well I don't like to point fingers."

This is known as "gaslighting", the denying of another's perceived reality, and it is very toxic and maddening. But denial, while it works in direct opposition to the truth and the actual position, has its function for the addict. Their furtiveness makes them less likely to get caught and so they are able to continue in a situation which they don't really want to change since they are addicted to it and are blind to the pain it causes themselves and others. In any case, the addiction has its own force and momentum which it would take effort, and therefore pain, to reverse. So, we have three aspects to this clinical pattern: we have the addict for who addiction is king, but who, to add to the complexity, is invested in not admitting to the status quo, leading often to concealing and manipulative behaviours. Then there is the family member – you – who feels to blame. But now, in respect of this third point, we have an important question to ask.

WHY DO WE TAKE THE BLAME?

This question turns out to be simple to answer in some respects. We, as family members or invested friends, are only too willing to take the blame because if it is our fault, then we are responsible and this in turn means there is an opening to remain in control and fix the problem ourselves. Wouldn't that be nice? It would mean that to some extent the problem is located within our reach.

This in fact amounts to a sort of double denial. On the one hand, it contributes to our own failure to face the extent of the situation. But of course, this tendency to consider ourselves culpable also means that we prop up the addict's own denial – and in larger families, it is possible in fact to build a whole system whose very structure consists of a collective failure to acknowledge the reality of what has occurred.

It can be striking too how sometimes we think we might be facing up to the problem – when in fact our attempts are inadequate and perhaps simply designed to make us feel we have 'done something'. For instance, we might confront the addict in a way which feels momentous but which in fact is full of evasions and tiptoeing-around.

"I was really scared when you didn't come home last night. Were you, you know, doing anything?"

In this sort of dialogue, note the fear of being direct, of naming the fear and robustly confronting the behaviour. Namelessness is a secret power which addiction possesses, until it is pinpointed and diagnosed. When Macbeth comes upon the witches in Shakespeare's play, he asks what they are doing: "A thing without a name," comes the reply.

And how will the addict reply to this? "Oh for goodness' sake, will you ever stop? All you do is nag, nag, nag. It's like living in the F-ing Soviet Union being around you. I work f-ing hard all day and I'm entitled to some r and r, and if I *had* taken something who would blame me with a wife/husband/

mother/father/daughter brother (delete as appropriate) like you! What's it got to do with you anyway?"

Theses sort of misfiring exchanges will plunge the whole relationship into denial. After a confrontation fails in this manner, it makes it unlikely that a confrontation will be attempted again for a little while: it establishes a pattern which is difficult to break. The threads of addiction become impossible to unpick. Life becomes entirely misshapen, like living in a palace of distorting mirrors in which the addiction holds sway and dictates the conditions of reality.

Once the addiction has the whip hand over the central relationship in the household like this, then it is on course to spread into the wider family, infecting all relationships. Family life becomes like living under a tyrannical regime, with a terrible set of lies at its centre: that the addict is not an addict and that accordingly the addict is not at fault. Soon secrets abound; people begin to operate according to private assumptions which they don't have the confidence to air; suspicions about the true situation are suppressed or diverted; soon, because there is no safe space in which to come together and discuss reality, each family member acquires a separate agenda, and the family becomes split, usually without at first suspecting that something so dramatic, and seemingly final, has occurred.

Once the family becomes aware of it, and there is a drive towards therapy, there is a strong sense of having to get things "right", as if there is a certain prescribed method that will resolve issues and get the family back on track, although what that track might be is less than clear by this point. In my experience, what usually happens is that there is an obscure sense among everybody in the family – with the likely exception of the addict – that something is broken, that there is unrealised potential in the family. Of course in some cases, these realisations might manifest in a more extreme way: the majority of the family may feel that life has become unbearable. But it is far more typical than one might suppose for there to be a kind of pervasive mystification in the family system. Due to the subterfuge of the addict, and the subtle way in which denial has spread throughout the family unit, families can seem oddly unable to place their finger on the nature of the problem. They begin using words like 'should', 'must', and 'ought' – but in general terms, unaware of the precise source of the problem. Everybody is subject to a sort of grief which cannot be removed, precisely because it cannot be located.

Shouldn't life be better than this? Must we always be arguing? Oughtn't we be doing something different?

THE BREAKDOWN OF THE SYSTEM

These are sure signs that the problem is being externalised, that we are turning away from the predicament of the addict – which ought to be the central question – into a world of easy fixes.

Worse, we tend not to agree on what that fix might be. Every family member believes that some sudden stroke can fix the problem. All at once, everybody somehow seems to acquire a different set of mythical rules, and begins to try to impose them on the other members. Each person is in fact completely ill-equipped to deal with the real situation and so everybody levels simple solutions at the problem. Dad believes common sense, a decent job and discipline are what is required. Mum argues that love, compassion and tolerance will somehow win the addict over. Meanwhile, Brother has acquired the view that the parents should throw the addict out.

This, then, is the image of a family at war. It is split into factions, almost as much addicted to its own secret interpretations now as the addict is to their addiction. Everybody is ashamed, angry and resentful. The life of the family shrinks and withers, and becomes unmanageable both internally and externally. Happiness has fled; it feels a remote memory. Externally, friends drift away due to lack of communication, social lives narrow and close down, resources meant for other things are diverted into the addiction. Sensible financial reasoning can go completely out of the window: "If I pay off his debts, then he will have less stress and will be better able to look after himself." Or: "We've cancelled our holidays this year so the money can go towards getting her a flat of her own."

This sort of reasoning will seem bizarre, but in my experience it is really the tip of the iceberg in terms of what families will convince themselves of in relation to addiction. I have had a parent ask me where they can buy the "very best" cocaine in the tortured belief that if they buy the best it is safer and then they will be able to stop their daughter prostituting herself to obtain the stuff.

But whatever set of ruses comes into play, emotions have become unmanageable. Nobody in the family really knows how to cope. Accordingly, extreme anxiety floods the domestic atmosphere. By a horrible logic, anger and resentment leak out into every situation and toxic shame shuts down all other feelings and begins, inexorably, to extinguish self-belief and love. Trust becomes impossible. It has been betrayed so many times and yet still we cling to the forlorn hope that if we just love and trust the addict enough, they will see a glimmer of light.

But everything keeps coming back to the core problem: as I said at the beginning, the addict loves the drink, drug or behaviour much more than they love you and the family. That relationship is their *primary relationship* and overriding organising principle. It is what the addict thinks about first thing in the morning, whilst they are taking their first shower, while they are eating their breakfast and so it goes on, morning, noon and night. Every minute is taken up with planning their addiction, fantasising about it, procuring the opportunity to further it, and, in their own way, recovering from their latest bout of it so that the whole cycle can begin again.

In short, everybody is going about their business unaware of the true nature of the problem, its ungovernable persistence and power. They use previous reference points which they have used in other situations to fix this.

They assume logic will win the day. The first thing addicts and their families need to do then is to name the problem and understand it better.

ON THE CHRONIC NATURE OF ADDICTION

We have stated earlier that the addict loves their addiction more than anything and that all else is now secondary to them – and often a very distant second indeed. But it is now necessary to delve into the sheer intractability of what we are discussing in these pages.

When I am working with addicts who might be thinking about their need to address their condition, I may ask them to compare their situation with someone suffering with another potentially life-threatening condition – a heart problem perhaps.

That's because addiction is a chronic condition, albeit one of a peculiar kind which means we do not typically see it for what it is. In the treatment of addiction there is no debilitating medication or chemotherapy, no oncologist to suggest yet another drug that might give you another six months of life. There is no life-changing surgery. In fact, the situation is rather black and white: follow one road and your life will improve beyond measure - but follow the other and the entire fabric of your existence will unravel and you will likely end up alone and in great emotional pain. It is, as they say, a no-brainer.

We all feel this ought not to be happening to us, and to our loved one, and so we make excuses. Please do not imagine that because your loved one went to Oxford or Cambridge – or because you live in the Cotswolds, or Jane Austen country or Harrogate or Dulwich Village – that you are somehow above all this. I have worked with tramps, prisoners, businessmen, opera singers, surgeons and princes in my career and must report that the disease cares not one jot for your social status: it can inflict itself on any system anywhere.

This sense of the power of addiction is both alarming to admit and in another sense freeing. It allows us to absolve ourselves and turn our attention to the actual problem.

What is striking is the sheer range of people who suffer from addiction. I was once asked to work with an extraordinarily wealthy gentleman somewhere in Saudi. I shall not elaborate for reasons of confidentiality. He was suffering with a chronic cocaine dependency that was seriously impacting not only his mental health, but his physical health as well; he was developing a heart problem as a consequence. His family, of course, were deeply concerned and offered to pay me very well. However, I felt I had to refuse. Why on earth would you do that? I hear you ask. Well, you see, he was using a great deal of cocaine, and cocaine of a very high quality. He was also very likely being charged well over the odds, as money to him was not a real issue. I had to wonder how the person who was supplying the drug would feel about some unknow westerner infidel killing their cash cow. It occurred to me that the suppliers would likely be ruthless. I didn't wish to be beheaded, and so I declined.

In stark contrast, for a while I worked in a street agency in Rotherham, Yorkshire. Rotherham is on the borders of what one might call the Badlands of England. Southeast Yorkshire was once a thriving mining and steel-making community with a deep sense of tradition and a rich culture. It was a place with its own songs, stories and values, all of which had become a way of life for several generations. When Scargill and Thatcher – for no reason other than vanity and the need to be right – between them destroyed this community, it was as if the region had somehow lost its soul. Men felt useless and the women, resentful and ashamed. Anxiety and depression increased dramatically, especially among the male population. With the usual mechanical disregard for detail, doctors began prescribing an SNRI, called venlafaxine, an anti-anxiety antidepressant. One of the main side effects of this drug is male impotence.

In the agency I worked with, a group of largely men – who had had all hope taken from them – became addicted to something called Musical Milk. Musical Milk was fifty percent white star cider and fifty percent surgical spirit. It was a difficult and desperate task, the main thrust of which was attempts to get those about to die of alcoholic poisoning into the local A&E. But then I have also sat with princes, distraught because their father's accountant has just told them they need to save money by using commercial aeroplane flights instead of chartering 747s. I have also known men serving life sentences for murders of which they have no recollection because they were in drug and alcohol induced blackout; the wives of City financiers who are in shock because they have learned only this morning that their £5 million pound dream home is repossessed to pay off their husbands gambling debts and they have to move out, with their children in a matter of hours. Addiction is everywhere. It doesn't care where you live, whether you are prince or pauper, what public school you went to or what state school you were expelled from at thirteen, what you believe about addiction, who your great grandfather was, whether you are Christian, Muslim or one of Zarathustra's magi. Anyone is eligible.

THE RECOVERY PROCESS

So, what happens if the addict is propelled by some sort of intervention to get themselves into what is known as recovery – that mysterious, exclusive, and seemingly incomprehensible realm wherein the addict is king or queen?

Recovery – and especially early recovery – is a bewildering thing because in that context addiction is still the organising principle of the family, albeit recovery from addiction. Sometimes, I wonder if people realise what an incremental improvement it is for the family to enter into the recovery process. However good it might feel to be finally in a clinical setting, families need to realise that the emphasis is almost exclusively on the addicted individual with little thought given to the equally important recovery of the family members and of the system. There is, unfortunately, a culture of false nobility surrounding early recovery. Often the addict goes from chaotic horror to self-righteous evangelist much to the confusion of the family who are so anxious that they feel compelled to go along with this and buy into the addict's "noble struggle". This needs to be challenged. What is so praiseworthy about beginning to stop being self-centred, angry, abusive, manipulative, and dishonest?

In some ways, responsibility for this might lie within the addiction treatment community, who for reasons best known to themselves have elevated the recovery process from an illness to a quest for enlightenment. I well remember my early years of recovery – and I mean years, the recovery process is longer than you may have been led to believe. In hindsight, it took me a good three years to begin to recognise and come to terms with how insane I had been and how much hurt I had caused others. I now recognise that I probably had an emotional age of about twelve, had no idea of how to be in the world and was so afraid and self-centred as to be almost a danger to myself. I had no concept of such things as paying rent, paying bills, compassion, relationships with others that weren't just about me and concern for others. It took time for me as "I" to emerge from the emotional carbonite of addiction. It might be more appropriate to regard treatment centres as nurseries for adults. There is a saying in AA that goes: "If you take the alcohol out of alcoholism you are left with the ISM, which stands for I'm Still Mad!"

For me, the key to this is in the AA Big Book where Bill Wilson states that this programme is a 'bridge to normal living'. To be equitable, these early attitudes of the addict are a normal part of what is called Post-Acute Withdrawal and can be a positive sign; however, it is neither useful nor necessary for the whole family to be dragged into the addict's worldview yet again. Instead, the family as a whole needs to recover for their own sakes. Of course, this begs the question "What is 'normal'?" What applies in the Serengeti may be entirely inappropriate in Lewisham. If I may speak from my own experience, 'normal' meant having a clear idea of where I would sleep tomorrow, the day after and next month. It meant a very basic routine of mealtimes, getting up and going to bedtimes – and, later on, a routine that included work. 'Normal' was no longer being tossed into a sea of nothingness and noise, of slowly recovering from the huge shipwreck of my life and my own esteem. Clean clothes, showers, regular meals and most important, a gradual emerging from the wracking pains of guilt, shame, and anger. For me this was normal and felt unreachable. For the family, it may be the gradual restoration of normal relations; of beginning to reclaim the everyday elements and roles of family life – and daring to hope that a real change, a metanoia can come about.

In an ideal world, it would be better to separate addict and family for a year and get them to work on their own recoveries. In my experience, the whole family system needs to recover from this illness. There really ought to be a parallel recovery process for families. The Twelve Steps apply just as much to the family as to the addicted member and I thoroughly recommend that family members weave the timeless wisdom of the steps into their lives – as I shall discuss in more detail later in this book.

SEPARATING THE ADDICT FROM THE DISEASE

Is addiction a disease? This is a question which is often asked, and I'm not entirely sure it matters.

What matters is that all persons concerned come to recognise that addiction is not a condition of identity. It is not about who you are as a human, it is something that you suffer with whether you are an addicted person or family member. Dis-identifying with the addiction is an essential part of the recovery process and if seeing it as a disease or an illness helps that – well then, all well and good.

What's also important is that we shy away from the "self-inflicted" argument – often held by successful late middle-aged men. This argument tends to run in the opposite direction to the 'disease' argument and is likely to be very harmful. If we state that the addiction is all the addict's fault, we can then end up arguing that we shouldn't 'let the addict off the hook' and permit them to abdicate responsibility. I can assure you that trying to help from that perspective will cause havoc, both with the addict and in the family system. It is an attitude which will only promote resentment, shame-splitting and faction-forming within the system, and will lead to fracture and secrecy where what is urgently required is cohesion and transparency.

But in truth it doesn't matter precisely how we define addiction, so for the sake of argument let's call it a disease. This allows us to separate from the addiction and thereby have some resources with which to begin to tackle the difficulties. One cannot pick up a plank of wood on which one is standing. If we call it a disease, it allows us to see it as a discreet thing, an "it" with which we can struggle. The virtues of this approach are quite clear. Who do you want in control of your life? Do you want it to be You – the person that you actually are?

Or do you want it to be It – the anxious, angry reactive thing that addiction has transmogrified you into?

This "It" warrants some further investigation. There are many ways to look at It; it could be described as the metabolic brain or the reptile brain. It might be referred to as undeveloped essence, the unconscious with its deterministic drives or the id, as the Freudians would have it. There is some utility in all of these descriptions, but whichever way we look at It, one thing remains. It is powerful and It wants to feed itself to the exclusion of the development of your actual and better self.

THE ONUS IS ON YOU

So let's be clear what the situation is. The three Cs of the Al-Anon programme are really valuable and contain a depth of implicit wisdom if they can be taken to heart and put into practice. They are:

You didn't **Cause** It.
You can't **Control** It.
You can't **Cure** It.

There you have it: reality in three short sentences. But perhaps a little surprisingly, many family members find this very difficult to accept. They believe that intelligence, reason, kindness and whatever else must surely prevail and of course it is a family's place to help, support and nurture its members come what may. But as we have begun to see throughout this chapter, kindness, love and understanding will not ultimately shift the problem. The chances are that if you are reading this you have already done everything you can think of, possibly many times over, to no avail and have now fallen into vague repetition of the same behaviours. And you're doing this in the forlorn hope that somehow magically things might change.

Well, magically they just might. In this book, I will ask that you take the focus off the addict in your life and place it firmly on yourself. So very often I hear from a newcomer at a family support group "I'm here for my husband/son/daughter/partner/ whatever and to learn how I can best support them".

This book has none of that: it isn't about them. It is squarely and unequivocally about you and your part in the whole horrible mess.

Exercise 1

Make a list of all your life roles. This includes things like Father, Sister, Wife, Employee, Friend, Godmother even as far down as golfing companion or tennis partner. Be as detailed and as thorough as you can; you can't really do too much.

Once you are satisfied with this list, take one example and reflect on how it has been affected by another's addiction. For example, how has a son's alcoholism usurped the father's chance to be a loving guide, mentor and ally? How has addiction corrupted the relationship to such an extent that what should be sweet is now bitter and what should be nourishing is now poisonous? In other words, what has addiction stolen from you?

Apply this process to as many of your life roles as you can. This will give you a sense of the toxic power of addiction and how it can take over not just the life of the addicted individual – but the whole family system and beyond.

Dark Sun:

A New Approach to Families and Addiction

CHAPTER TWO

ADDICTION AS A SPIRITUAL DISEASE

A man is walking home late one night when he sees an anxious Mulla Nasrudin down on all fours, crawling on his hands and knees on the road, searching frantically under a streetlight for something on the ground.
"Mulla, what have you lost?" the passerby asks.
"I am searching for my key," Nasrudin says worriedly. "I'll help you look," the man says and joins Mulla Nasrudin in the search. Soon, both men are down on their knees under the streetlight, looking for the lost key. After some time, the man asks Nasrudin, "Tell me Mulla, do you remember where exactly did you drop the key?" Nasrudin waves his arm back toward the darkness and says, "Over there, in my house. I lost the key inside my house..." Shocked and exasperated, the passer-by jumps up and shouts at Mulla Nasrudin, "Then why are you searching for the key out here in the street?" "Because there is more light here than inside my house," Mulla Nasrudin answers nonchalantly.

Case History 2

Part of my role as an addiction therapist is to hold a mirror to the seriousness of the situation. The denial attached to what amounts to a global pandemic of drugs is staggering. It's something which most people don't see, no doubt because it is an extremely unpleasant fact about our life today. You might hear on the news that 500 kilograms of cocaine with a street value of £8 million were seized in a raid in Hull, but that is about all. You may not know that huge areas of rainforest are being cleared to make way for cocaine growing, that the annual income across the world from illicit heroin and cocaine runs into the hundreds of billions of dollars, that the WHO statistics have alcoholism as the biggest killer on the planet.

In 2015 and 2016, I was working in Karachi, Pakistan. I was there helping to train therapists – mainly women – in addiction treatment. In all honesty, they did more to train me than I them, but I did what I could. These women were working to help feral street children, who were perhaps between the ages of seven and nine, and who had one thing in common: they were addicted to heroin. Accordingly, they were all beggars, although they did not keep anything they gleaned, and many of them were child prostitutes. These children were run by gangs – unscrupulous and callous organisations who kept the young ones on the edge of heroin withdrawal, which made them compliant and obedient. Helmand Province in Afghanistan is not very far from Karachi, and heroin is both plentiful and cheap. The women therapists had almost no resources and no training at all: they did whatever they could to try to help. They were remarkable souls.

I tell you this, and I could say a lot more, to get across how widespread and tragic addiction is and how little notice seems to be taken of it. You may say, "Yes, but this isn't Karachi, something so horrible as that surely can't happen here in England?" However prosperous and comforting this little Island may seem, I wouldn't be too sure of that…

THE STRANGENESS OF IT ALL

Addiction is a strange business. Many times, I have facilitated a family support group in which the topic inevitably and inexorably, like some doomed planet pulled into a black hole, reverts to talking about *them*, meaning the addict in their lives. This is fascinating because downstairs, in another part of the building there is likely an aftercare group for the addicted folks who have recently left treatment. I can assure you that they will be talking exclusively about *themselves* also without even a passing thought as to horrors that their loved ones might have been through at the hands of addiction.

This sort of thing is symptomatic of addiction and is a clear sign of the grip it has on the system. The gravitational pull is, in effect, only one way: everybody, including the addict, only talks, thinks, analyses, or ponders the addict. The plight of everyone else has been ruthlessly backgrounded by the addiction. What is going through your mind as you are reporting every detail of their behaviour over the past weeks? As we saw in the last chapter, you are examining, Sherlock Holmes-like, every minute detail in the hope of unearthing some shred of hope, or some clue as to how you might change and adapt in order to fix their condition. You are only reinforcing the illusion of control as a means of avoiding the real pain of what is going on. We have already seen that this amounts to a subtle form of denial.

But there is a way out. It will involve realising that you are as much a part of the problem as the identified addict. By owning your part and by taking real responsibility you will not only improve the quality of your own life but will be able to change the dynamic of the system in such a way as to allow the oxygen of recovery to flood in and rejuvenate an otherwise asphyxiating situation.

ENTER THE BROTHERS GRIMM

It is my conviction that the collected Fairy Tales – they should really be called Wonder Tales as they rarely feature fairies – contain fragments of a lost and valuable wisdom. Take for example the tale called 'The Water of Life'.

It begins with a dying King who is told by an old man that the only cure for his ills is the Water of Life, but that it is very hard to find indeed. In this story, the King has three sons, and the elder two brothers have a conviction that they know better than their father what is best for them. If you read the story, you will see that that didn't end well for them. But for the younger son, a different path is taken, towards the miraculous, and as we shall see, this is the path which the family system must take in order to encounter a new and hopeful set of structures. We must read stories like this with interest and delight, because great wisdom is there to help us in whatever situation we happen in. It might also be that when we are caught up in the terrible behaviour loops of addiction, we must seek help wherever we can find it.

When it comes to 'The Water of Life', we can see intriguing parallels with the addicted family system. Typically, the family is held in thrall by a set of beliefs which keep it sick and are slowly killing it. The hope for a cure lies in something almost miraculous and outside the frame of reference of the status quo. However this cure is hard won and involves a journey, and all journeys are both external – in this case involving wonderful encounters with dwarves, castles and princesses – but also internal, asking us to reimagine ourselves. One recurring motif of these stories is the necessary interaction between two worlds – two interdependent levels of being – each needing the other to fulfil purpose and achieve healing and release. In folklore across the world, the quotidian and the miraculous appear to be somehow bound up. The other world in Grimm is often called "The Forest Behind The Mountain Where The Fox and The Hare say Goodnight". In Russia it is known as Faraway Tsaradom, or The Thrice Times Nine land, where a domineering princess reigns and Stravinsky's famous firebird is to be found. In Ireland, it is Tír na nÓg, an island paradise of supernatural beauty. In Britain it is the Avalon of Arthurian legend. It is a matter of great interest that these places recur in the stories which really matter to us, and which seem to come from some deep place within the human psyche. Shambala, Lyonesse, Brigadoon: these places recur, and while at this stage in our narrative, it isn't necessary to delve too deeply into what the presence of these Wonder Tales in our literature might mean, it is important to lay them down as markers within your experience: to realise at this early stage in this book that there is in your midst something which you may have almost ceased to believe in – and that is hope. By this I don't mean any vague abstract noun – but a genuine place of peace and reconciliation which you might, even in your present painful predicament, definitely arrive at and live in one day. The above is especially important because for the family caught up in the spirals of addiction, there is a very serious problem when it comes to facing up to what you are likely facing if you are reading this book.

AN INFURIATING LACK OF INFORMATION

When we are in a difficult situation, we have first to orient ourselves and try to find a path. We have already seen in Chapter One how addiction has a cunning tendency to hide and conceal itself. Its principal trait is secrecy; this allows it to prosper in a terrible variety of ways and wreak havoc on the family system, often before anyone in the family has even begun to intuit that there's a problem at all. It steals a march on us.

It is partly because of this that there is such a terrible poverty of help for those who are thrust into the perils of addiction. None of the usual channels of help and information are really of any use. We have seen huge gains in our understanding of cancer and heart ailments in the past 50 years. But when it comes to the rife miseries of addiction, we find dry wells, and deceptive paths which lead us in circles. Few doctors are given any proper training on this subject; psychiatrists are poorly informed; and the NHS has almost nothing to offer, and indeed will often turn away an addiction sufferer. Not only then does addiction do considerable damage without detection, but we have no means of catching up once we do begin to suspect what is going on.

To compound matters, as we saw in the last chapter, the family will know little about the terrible reality with which they are dealing. Accordingly, when a psychiatrist offers a two-week inpatient detox at a suitable establishment, they jump at the chance and often feel – misguidedly, I'm afraid – that their troubles are over and tomorrow will be nothing but roses. But in the majority of cases, the detox is simply not enough. In fact, I can safely say that when faced with addiction, two weeks' treatment is never sufficient. In fact, none of the usual ruses tend to work, medication, one-one psychotherapy, meditation, spiritual retreats, spas, new girlfriends, world cruises – I have seen all these remedies attempted and I am afraid with extremely limited success. Why do these strategies fail? For the simple reason that the addict isn't really committed to genuine change.

The reality is that three to six months is a reasonable period of treatment, although even here, this raises a particular concern. There is a myth that an addict has to Really Want To Stop before any treatment is likely to prove effective. This is not the case. In the right environment and surrounded by an appropriate culture, a person may acquire the desire for real change – what I have called in the previous chapter, a metanoia. However, because of the reality of denial which I also outlined in Chapter One, and because of pervasive ignorance about the true nature of addiction, I have found that this length of treatment is met with dismay by the families of addicts, and by addicts themselves. *Six months! Surely this is a gigantic overreaction.* But really, we need to think about addiction in the same way as we would any life-threatening condition: if an oncologist were to suggest the same length of treatment, you probably wouldn't think twice. But unfortunately, an addict will very often seize upon a short-term or softer option just to get the family off their backs. Give them a choice of three months' inpatient treatment or a year's weekly psychotherapy, which won't work anyway, and watch what happens.

I once had a private practice in Harley Street, London. A lady had called me asking if I would see her husband for a course of therapy. With many reservations I agreed to at least see the fellow for an assessment. He was a late middle-aged gentleman. He had been a barrister and had recently retired. As the session progressed, my first thoughts were confirmed. As soon as I saw him, I knew by his physical appearance that he had an advanced problem and might even be approaching what is called the pre-morbid stage. As we talked, he reluctantly revealed at least a degree of the extent of his drinking. As I usually do in these circumstances, I cautiously tried to make him aware of the seriousness of his situation and the need for immediate treatment. Of course, he told me I was overreacting, being melodramatic and that he didn't drink any more that his chums at the golf club (stereotypical I know, but stereotypes have roots in reality). For myself, I considered perhaps after a few more sessions he would see some glimmer of sense, perhaps his GP would caution him, or something might happen to wake him a little. He agreed to more sessions, remarking that his wife would be pleased. Each session was the same. He earnestly avoided talking of anything that might matter, and always dragged the topic towards what was going on in the news or the unnecessary holiday his wife was planning. I have to be honest: I was struggling to like the fellow and began to dread his sessions. Then it became clear to me. I had allowed myself to become part of the problem. In seeing me, he was keeping his wife at bay without having to contemplate change. Meanwhile, his wife felt that at last something was being done, he was now able to say that he was dealing with his problem without having to deal with his problem. At the next session, I straightaway told him that I was unable to help him any further and that in my professional opinion he needed urgent inpatient treatment if he wanted to live beyond fifty five. He stormed out muttering "nonsense" and "American psychobabble" as he went.

Meanwhile, in another part of the galaxy, I was approached by the mother of a twenty year old man, let's call him Jake, hopelessly addicted to heroin and completely out of control. His mother was in a turmoil of anxiety and expected to find out he was dead at any time. Jake had previously attended rehab, but seemingly to no avail. The psychiatrist he had been under refused to treat him further because he was abusing any prescribed medication. I told Jake's mother there was likely nothing I could do on a one-to-one basis, but had she considered the possibility of an intervention? Now, I need to say at this point that I do not like doing interventions – but sometimes, just sometimes, they can work. I talked Jake's mother through the process and she agreed to try it.

So at an agreed time and place, five or six friends and family gathered with their pre-written intervention letters.

I should explain here. An intervention letter is a quite specific thing and it is about the person writing the letter and not about the addicted individual. These letters are in three parts, the first is of specific occasions where the writer has felt love, joy, pride or any other positive emotion towards the addict. There should be three examples. The next part is of times when you have seen the true terror of the addict's situation. It doesn't matter if these provoke shame: that is, in fact, the intent. Again, there should be three of these. The last part is about asking the addict to get help and the consequences of them refusing that request.

So all were gathered and Jake arrived. He was, as they always are, very taken aback but he agreed to hear the letters. It was a highly charged and emotional process, but it had the desired effect. Jake agreed to go to treatment for at least eight weeks. He spent the night at the family home, under close guard, and the next morning he was on his way to rehab. Eight weeks later, he was on a train home, and he got drunk. His mother, meeting him at the station, took one look at Jake and turned her back on him. This effected a sea change for Jake. After a few homeless days during which he managed to neither drink nor use drugs, Jake contacted his mother and apologised.

This was three years ago. Jake is now in recovery and has been since his last relapse. He is working, helping other addicted individuals and has his own flat.

Any therapist that knows about addiction will always recommend group therapy over one-to-one, and inpatient treatment as the preferred path. If you are offering help to an addicted loved one, don't allow them to choose where they go. They will get on the Internet and find places that offer results in ten days, or they will find establishments which promise a return to social drinking and recreational drug use: I'm afraid such snares do exist, which take

advantage of the general uncertainty and lack of knowledge in our society surrounding addiction. Let us then do a little debunking to assist in this process.

THE PHYSICAL, THE MENTAL AND THE SPIRITUAL

The Big Book of Alcoholics Anonymous names alcoholism – and by
association all addiction – as a physical, mental and spiritual disease.

What might this mean? The first thing to say is that addiction, in whatever form, exists in the person and not in the substance. Contrary to widespread belief, one does not become an addict through taking drugs nor an
alcoholic by drinking vast amounts of booze. The reverse is true: one takes
drugs because one suffers with addiction, and one drinks to excess because
one is suffering with alcoholism. This is not just about physical dependency
although that is significant and needs to be addressed, rather it is about a
painful spiritual dependency in which the person is actually unable to stop.
The predisposition for this condition is there before descent into active, using
addiction takes place and it would not be awry to say that a significant number
of addicts are born like this. Immediately the question comes, "Is it genetic?".
That is not a useful question and a rabbit hole down which we could disappear
for the rest of this book. It depends too much on definitions and I intend this
to be a practical book. I therefore suggest we take each factor separately and
examine it in a little depth.

From a physical point of view, we can assume that there is a specific
physiology with a particular set of chemicals attached to this condition. This
amounts to physical predisposition, but I'm afraid to say it doesn't get us very
far to point this out. That's because though there is a clear physical component
to this condition, at time of writing there is no meaningful medical response
to this illness – no pill, no surgery, no course of antibiotics or anti-depressants
that will address the situation. Addicts seek to become numb, and modern
psychiatric medicine will only add to an already perilous spiritual torpor. It

is another example of the way in which medicine, so sophisticated in a range of other illnesses, is far behind in this one.

In fact, I'm afraid that in my experience medicine often makes addiction worse. For example, a person suffering with alcoholism may present to their GP with depression and anxiety. The GP, rushed off their feet, prescribes a generic anti-depressant – which will have little effect as long as the person continues to drink – and the real difficulty is masked and hidden behind a more acceptable façade. Of course, if the enlightened GP enquires into the patient's drinking habits, the person will likely seek out another, more "understanding" doctor. It is very difficult, if not impossible, to diagnose accurately a concurrent psychiatric condition if drugs and alcohol are in the picture. At least six weeks of complete abstinence are necessary before any diagnosis can be made with confidence.

All drugs, including alcohol, are psycho-mimetic in that they will engender the apparent symptoms of other conditions including psychosis: very often, the drinking or drug-taking are the direct cause of depression and anxiety. This is another way in which addiction, with a sort of devil's cunning, manages to hide from the light of genuine treatment. A parent, partner or family member may very well prefer a diagnosis of depression or anxiety, because it will seem to them somehow more acceptable, more wholesome and more in keeping with the family belief system. The addicted family member will also prefer this way of proceeding as it will feel they have evaded detection and can continue drinking or taking their drug of choice. It is entirely possible that, because of the chronic lack of information and understanding out there in the world, the interminable round of doctors, specialists, psychiatrists, psychotherapists, shamans and faith healers will drag on and on, draining finances and emotional resources without tangible progress. For the situation to begin to improve at all, the crocodile nearest the boat, the addiction, needs to be faced and dealt with.

I will always robustly challenge the theory that addiction is caused by or is a symptom of childhood trauma of one kind or another, although it would be foolish of me to deny the impact of trauma upon the hope of a good treatment outcome. Here, I fall somewhat out of step with the likes of Gabor Mate and Johann Hari. While I would never deny that trauma is a powerful factor in addiction, treating it as a cause is, in my experience, less than useful and indeed may be the wide gate and broad way that leads to destruction. Of course, trauma is a chronic pain that must be treated – but not too soon. I have sat in many a therapy group with people struggling to recover from the demon of addiction and I can say that if you give them the chance to divert into trauma, and into explorations of childhood or transgenerational pathology, they will lean on that as something that needs to be dealt with before they can think about stopping drink or drugs. *Why* has no utility. Knowing the make of pistol and the calibre of the bullet does little to help the person who has been shot. Another serious danger of treating trauma too soon is that something may be unleashed that the patient is not able to deal with at that time. This is particularly true of some kinds of sexual abuse. Very often, such dreadful experiences have been buried – and buried for good reason. Stripping the psyche of its defences too quickly and too soon may prove catastrophic. One might call this the mental aspect of the horrid trinity of addiction. It is the carried shame, anger, resentment and fear that drag the addict and the family into the descent to Avernus.

There is then, the spiritual pillar. When it is suggested that addiction is a spiritual malaise what does that mean? Is it brought on by inadequate or reluctant attendance at chapel or church? Is it some kind of divine retribution for a life of sin? I couldn't tell you. And yet, at root, addiction is a spiritual disease, an affliction brought on by a great disconnection with the underlying good of the universe. Of course, in one form or another, this disease is as old as mankind. Yet the way we see it now – ubiquitous, normalised, and ever more deadly – is relatively modern. Fairly recently in historical terms something happened that changed the world in a way as never before: it was a sort of historical singularity. Its seed was sown in the Reformation and the Renaissance when science and reason parted company with spirituality. These seeds bore the fruit that became known as the Industrial Revolution, the beginning of the so-called modern world. In a range of catastrophic ways, humankind went about disconnecting itself from itself, from nature and from any sense of cosmic belonging. All this is at the root of the current accelerating pandemic of addiction. The processes of education, medicine, religion and of all the other western institutions, became as machines and we human beings fell into a trance and became mechanical in response. I shall be enlarging upon this theme in a moment.

ADDICTION AND THE BRAIN STRUCTURE

What, then, is the pathogen associated with addiction? In my experience the most useful model states that the hormone cortisol is the primary antagonist. It is a steroid in the glucocorticoid class of hormones. When you open the curtains of a lovely sunny morning, your adrenals will begin the production of this steroid and you will begin to wake up. To say cortisol is a stress hormone is perhaps a little misleading. It is very necessary and we cannot function without it: we need optimum levels of cortisol to maintain an optimum level of positive stress during our waking hours. However, if the levels of cortisol are chronically high – and especially if they are high over inappropriate lengths of time – something quite nasty starts to occur. In such cases, the sufferer begins to carry within themselves a sense of existential dread. This anxiety is not experienced cognitively, there is no rational explanation, rather it is felt in the pit of the stomach and is generalised as: "I am alone in a hostile universe. At any moment something bad will happen and I am not equipped to deal with it." This is the worldview of the addict and it is there from an early age, even birth. Many parents have reported to me that their afflicted son or daughter has always been somewhat "other" – by which they will usually mean anxious, compulsive or obsessive to a noticeable degree. This tendency, which won't necessarily lead to addiction, is too common in addiction to be ignored.

For the sake of this discussion, let's say that human beings have three brains, or centres, and for ease of distinction, let's categorise them in an evolutionary way. At the front of the brain, in the cerebrum, is the frontal cortex. Here is reason and meaning, ethics and morals, beliefs and personality. We might call this the human brain. Were we to subject an addicted individual to a brain scan and give them a hit of their favourite substance, we would see this area go dark, as if a switch had been thrown. The person that you know and love is no longer there and something much deeper and I have to say darker has taken their place.

Further back, in the cerebellum, we find the limbic or emotional brain. We can call this the mammal brain, as it happens to be the centre of being for the higher mammals such as dogs and horses. This brain is fast, somewhat remote and tends towards autonomy; in other words we can say we have little control over how our emotions might arise. The limbic system is also more powerful that the human brain. The sense of smell is directly connected to the limbic brain and we have all had the experience of an unexpected perfume or smell triggering an upsurge of powerful emotions and memories.

Now we come to the nub of the matter. Right at the back of the head, on top of and including the spinal column is the reptile or body brain. It is autonomous, we have little or no access to its workings. It regulates the electrolyte balance of the blood, digests our breakfasts, monitors and adapts heart rate, and administers body temperature in addition to a whole range of other functions. It is very powerful and has the capacity to override the entire organic system. If you want to test its power, try holding your breath for ten minutes. It is here in this metabolic centre that addiction takes a hold and that is what makes it such a tricky pest to deal with. That's because this brain is utterly self-centred: from its perspective, caught up entirely in internal processes, other people simply don't exist. It also operates on an extraordinarily short time frame: it minds only what happens in the next fifteen seconds, and it is primarily concerned with gratification and survival. This is known as the four F's of the crocodile brain and to recite these will involve me in a a slight lapse of tone. They are: Food, Flight, Fight and F**k. These might perhaps be best witnessed at a pub at closing time.

In general, you will note that when the reptile brain is most active, the human brain is in a state of atrophy. It is why when people are drunk, they tend not to discuss La Traviata or Shakespeare. Instead, they run from the police sirens, or lurch drunkenly towards the kebab shop, and make clumsy passes at one another. As we saw in the last chapter, the reptilian brain is rampant across all settings. A seemingly respectable dinner party may descend into tears and recriminations because the reptile brain has come to predominate, and the four Fs have become paramount for all participants. Sometimes this can seem comic and harmless enough and dealt with through a series of self-deprecating apologetic phone calls the following morning.

But in the instances under discussion, the situation is far more serious. We are not talking about just one night of misbehaviour, or the occasional binge – we are describing a hostile takeover of the human brain by the reptilian brain across the addict's whole existence.

This situation might unfold in the following way. You are at home with the addicted family member. All seems calm, and you are getting along pretty well. They tell you that they have an important meeting and need to "pop" out for a wee while. Several hours later they return home. You know immediately that something has changed and changed for the worse. They are surly, defensive, and aggressive. They might smell strange, and they are certainly behaving in a suspicious way. The person you know and love has disappeared and been replaced by a thing – an It – and it is simply not possible to have a relationship with It. It will take over. Before you know it, the addiction will become the organising principle of the family system. It will sit in the centre of the system, like a dark sun, controlling everyone by fear and dictating how everyone thinks, feels and behaves. Families fragment. Secrets become the norm. Splitting and factions arise where they were never before. Resentment, shame and anxiety become the only feelings available. It rules over all. It is hell really.

This then brings us to the crux of the difficulty. It isn't possible to have a normal human relationship with It. We are now able to say a little more than in the previous chapter about what It is – it's the reptilian brain. And we, the non-addicted, want to explore relationships through the human brain.

So let's repeat, knowing now a little more about the neuroscience behind this situation. The reptilian brain doesn't care about you or anyone else. It doesn't care, it just uses. It uses drink and drugs and behaviour, it uses people and you may be very sure that It will use you. Until the addicted family member begins to take responsibility for It and recognises the need for help and change, no amount of care, love, concern or compassion will have any effect other than in setting up a covert support system for the addiction. It is heart-breaking to see families trying to cope with addiction in the system; to watch the futile attempts at control, kindness, and care that will invariably get twisted into their very opposite by It.

What we are really watching is the human brain trying to interact with the reptilian – and the reptilian brain's refusal to reciprocate.

A BRIEF HISTORY OF ADDICTION

As we watch this, we are sadly observing an ancient misunderstanding – one with considerable and dreary pedigree. To know this is again to help us get the measure of what we are up against.

We can get a glimpse of the history of alcoholism through the arts and especially literature. Alcoholism crops up regularly in Chaucer, who famously observed that 'drunkenness is full of striving and misery'. It was as true then as now. Drink is a theme in Rabelais' work, and in that moralistic medieval poem *Piers Plowman*. In Falstaff, Shakespeare created a great character who is also an alcoholic, but it isn't always observed that Falstaff is embedded in an intricate moral framework which implicitly acknowledges that addiction exists in the person and not in the substance. Prince Harry in *Henry IV Parts I* and *II* drank and roistered with Falstaff but by the end of the play is able to turn away and grow up whereas Falstaff seemed unable to do the same. By *Henry V*, Prince Harry is now King, and we read of Falstaff's sad death. We sometimes read of Shakespeare as an amoral writer who makes no judgements, but I don't think this is quite as true as some people seem to think it is. It is quite clear from these plays that Shakespeare saw addiction for what it is: a rampant thing which destroys lives.

Then, in the centuries following Shakespeare, something happened: that historical singularity we mentioned earlier, which ushered in the so-called modern age, which also coincided with an enormous increase in addictive behaviours. What is a singularity? Really just that. Something that has never happened before. We tend to call this the Enlightenment, but that can be a misleading term since it led to a good deal of behaviour which can only really be characterised as dark. Imagine a Roman or an Ancient Briton suddenly transposed into Elizabethan England. Things would be very different in lots of respects: cathedral architecture, some scientific advances, larger cities. But the essential fabric of life would be the same. I expect the Roman or Ancient Brit would struggle at first but would probably be able to make sense of this new world – because the Elizabethans never wholly severed themselves with the past, as we sometimes seem to have done. If we shift those same ancients into Victorian England, we will find that something essential has changed, there are no longer the points of reference that allowed the ancients to begin to make sense of what is around them.

What they would struggle to understand would be the Disenchantment of the World. Life seemed somehow to have lost its charge, and its magic.

The scientific method gave us wonderful contraptions, of course, but it also led to a terrible internal emptiness which sent huge numbers of people into addictive behaviours to numb the pain. A confluence of certain ideas and theories occurred. Rene Descartes (1596-1650) would describe a fundamental division between mind and body: the so called Cartesian split. Isaac Newton (1642-1726) – interestingly, Newton was also an alchemist, and so a more complicated figure than we sometimes realise – proposed that the universe can be viewed and understood as a machine. Karl Marx (1818-1883) declared religion to be the opium of the people. Charles Darwin (1809-1882) propounded a competitive world engaged in a life and death struggle, which Richard Dawkins (1941-) in our own time would describe as the work of 'a blind watchmaker'. In time, Friedrich Nietzsche (1844-1900) would frame what is probably one of his most famous and misunderstood quotes:

"God is dead. God remains dead. And we have killed him. How shall we comfort ourselves, the murderers of all murderers? What was holiest and mightiest of all that the world has yet owned has bled to death under our knives: who will wipe this blood off us? What water is there for us to clean ourselves? What festivals of atonement, what sacred games shall we have to invent? Is not the greatness of this deed too great for us? Must we ourselves not become gods simply to appear worthy of it?"

This social and historical singularity fundamentally changed Western man's relationship with his world, leading to widespread disconnection and disenchantment. People became frightened – more frightened than before because the threat was now intangible. It was all a great disaster, vastly increasing the range of motives for entering into addictive patterns. The assault on truth came from every angle. Science and philosophy were presenting a mechanical world that seemed to all intents and purposes to be random and aloof. As if anxious to fall in line, all the fundamental institutions became mechanised. Medicine saw the human being as a machine and focused on the treatment of symptoms. Meanwhile, education became a conveyor-belt designed to churn out servants of the growing military industrial complex. Religion, especially Christianity began to be "de-natured". Relationship, which is essentially spiritual in nature, became mechanical and this created an ubiquitous existential dread that was reflected in the art and literature of the time. William Blake (1757-1827)'s famous poem 'Jerusalem' that is so often taken as a patriotic ode, is in fact an angry polemic against all that he saw happening. The English Romantics were writing apocalyptic visions, Mary Shelley (1797-1851) wrote *Frankenstein* (1818), Bram Stoker (1847-1912) wrote *Dracula* (1897). By reading these works we can gain a sense of how great the shift had been: it was as if the end of the world was nigh, and in the shapes of the First World War (1914-18) something truly terrible did occur.

But all along there had been terrible crises, which made people question the ultimate meaning of things. In 1815, The Volcano Mount Tamburo in Indonesia emitted the biggest volcanic eruption ever recorded. The eruption caused global climate anomalies in the following years, while 1816 became known as the year without a summer" due to the impact on North American and European weather. In the Northern Hemisphere, crops failed and livestock died, resulting in the worst famine of the century. This added to the overall sense of doom. The rise of centralised government enabled the Poor Laws to be passed with grave consequences. This meant there were increasing reasons to drink, and the British East India company would soon make that recourse much more affordable, changing the distillation laws, making the production of cheap liquor possible. All over London, stills arose producing cheap gin. But this was a global phenomenon: in America, rum was the drink of choice. Soon cocaine and opium were ubiquitous; by 1805 opium had been refined into morphine which seemed to find its way into a lot of cures, including Mrs Winslow's Soothing Syrup for teething infants – the chief ingredient of which was morphine. At this time disease was rife, poverty was everywhere, and one in four women made their living through prostitution. All in all, unless one were to some degree wealthy, things were quite ghastly.

It is an important thing therefore to consider one's historical inheritance. We live at a particular historical addiction moment – as everybody does, where the availability of alcohol and drugs has been long established. At the same time, the desirability of some sort of panacea for spiritual troubles has also arisen.

UPON CHILDHOOD

But the above is only part of the context in which addiction arises. The mental aspect of the disease of addiction as described by Bill Wilson has its provenance, as do so many things, in childhood.

At this point I should issue a warning to parents. You need to read this next part putting yourself in the position of the child. This is very important as I have come to discover that most parents of addicted persons are predisposed to self-blame and flagellation. This is neither true nor helpful and only increases the illusion of power and control. At this point also it is worth taking to heart again the mantra of the three Cs in our first chapter:

> You didn't **Cause** it
> You can't **Control** it
> You can't **Cure** it.

I often think that the deck is somewhat stacked against the creation of a healthy family system. This state of affairs is nobody's fault in particular. The overwhelming majority of parents with whom I come into contact do the very best they can with what they have. Do you remember the profound, detailed and extensive parenting lessons that you received at school? I thought not. I can vividly recall being given a great deal of information regarding Ox Bow

Lakes and something called The Diet of Worms, all of which didn't seem to have much relevance when my daughter was born. It is quite wrongly assumed that parents know how to raise a child and, most likely, they perform on their offspring a variation upon whatever was done to them.

It doesn't end there. Because of course there is the coven of grandparents and remote relatives who brim over with useful advice. *You should soak her feet in turpentine if she has diarrhoea. Wake him up every hour or he will get ringworm.* We are not educated in this but instead proceed blindly, doing our best, but with the vague suspicion that we are being asked to fly a jumbo jet without previous instruction.

No child comes into the world resentful, ashamed, anxious, and with low self-esteem. These negative belief systems are, in fact, quickly acquired by the child as they begin to interact with the outside world: the individual essence begins to learn the art of camouflage, of adapting as a means of survival. Before about aged seven, children are wonderful, magically limbic beings with a direct and unmodulated relationship with their world – a world of which they are the indisputable centre. Everything that happens in this world is about them. This is appropriate and as it should be. The parents are the Olympians of the child's world, the gods who cannot be wrong, for if the gods are wrong then the child is not safe and may be annihilated at any moment. Thus, if mother is angry, it is the fault of the child; if father leaves, it is because the child is not pretty, or clever or good enough. The child's frontal cortex wherein lies the ability to reason, to judge and to give meaning is not yet online, so to speak, and the dictum of the parents, the gods, is virtually downloaded directly into the child's psyche.

Pretty well everyone on the planet is hypnotised by some kind of developmental trauma and this trauma, as unlikely as it may sound is trans-generational: it is bequeathed from great-grandfather to grandfather, and thereon from father to son: research evidence in fact states that trauma stays in families for up to seven generations.

We ought to accept this context as a way of obtaining greater humility in ourselves, which ought in time to make it clear to us that we need to work not upon the addict in our lives but upon ourselves. But the scale of the inheritance in the addict's life also ought to help free us of the tendency to blame ourselves. We are, in effect, born into a vortex of unresolved trauma. But what is trauma, really?

ON NOT KEEPING TO THE SCRIPT

I definite trauma like this. All of us on this confused and bewildered little planet bring with us when we arrive here an essential self. This self is to be nourished and nurtured and shaped so that it may become a real human being. However, all too often, a new-born infant is handed a script and a contract by the family of origin system. The script is unequivocal and you don't get to negotiate whether you sign it – at least at first. It reads something like this:

This is who we need you to be, and this is what you will get if you follow the script.

None of us will remember the moment when we were handed this script, but the new arrival has to adapt to the unconscious and unspoken demands of the family system. By way of example, let's say a baby boy comes into a family where the father is a keen soccer player, though by no means professional standard. He picks up his new born son for the first time and, with genuine love, says something like: "There's my little Chelsea striker!" and begins to fantasise about all the unfulfilled wishes his son will fulfil for him. Whatever system a child is born into, an unconscious and implicit demand seems to be in place: the child must comply with the inherited and ancestral beliefs, principles, values, politics, religion and so forth of the family. What do "working class" "middle class" or "upper class" really mean? And what attitudes and worldviews go with those constructs? For that is all they are: social constructs that only have meaning in reference to the context that engendered them. This is really what I mean by 'trans-generational' and it is there right from the beginning even before the personal interactions of mother, father and siblings start to impact.

What is a child born into? Were they really wanted? Were they an unadmitted accident? Let's imagine a hypothetical scenario. Let's say Dad is a reasonably high up executive in a successful company in the early 1960s. He may have gone through the Second World War as a child and perhaps suffered the humiliation and abandonment of being an evacuee, or perhaps his father was a spitfire pilot killed in the Battle of Britain. Mum was his personal assistant. She too had gone through the war. Perhaps her family was Jewish and her father had escaped from a death camp, and made his way across Europe to safety in England. Whatever the facts, both mum and dad have provenance that stretches back into history and has, in all probability, been neither examined nor dealt with and so they are still carrying all sorts of systemic baggage. Let's now imagine that these two bright young things, on a business trip to Paris, have a liaison, and as an unwanted and unlooked for consequence of that liaison she falls pregnant.

What are they to do? Abortion is both unthinkable and illegal and single parenthood would cast them both into irredeemable opprobrium and probably cost them their careers. So they marry. They don't even properly know one another and yet they marry. He is thinking "How am I going to get out of this?" and she is thinking "My life is over!" The child, a little boy – let's call him Geoffrey – is born into this situation. The father gets a middle-of-the-road job and starts to work late, frequenting a pub popular with his work mates. He is often very late home – and, not infrequently, drunk. He becomes what is known as 'avoidant'. The mother has had to give up her career and is growing increasingly resentful and finds it more and more difficult to cope with Geoffrey. All around is a society and a family system that is covertly shaming.

You are supposed to want children and be happy when they arrive! She tries socialising with other young mothers but this only makes her feel worse.

And so we have a less than ideal situation. Geoffrey grows and develops in this atmosphere of shame and anger. In his sixth year, he is invited to the birthday party for the daughter of one of his father's directors. It now becomes important to make a good impression. The daughter's family are wealthy liberals who have a big house with a big garden, which even has a stream running through it. Mum and Dad buy an expensive gift for Geoffrey to take to the party. They buy him smart new clothes and a brand new pair of trainers. Geoffrey sets off for the party – and because the hosts are liberal and love children, he is allowed to run riot with the other kids and as a consequence ruins his new clothes. He returns home full of happiness and enthusiasm and rushes to tell mum all about the wonderful time he has had. Instead, he is met with: "Oh for goodness' sake, Geoffrey, look at the state of you! Have you any idea how much those clothes cost? Do you realise how very expensive those trainers were? What on Earth am I going to do with you? I'm at my wits' end already trying to cope and now this! Just wait until Dad gets home".

Dad comes home, rather late, but Geoffrey has had to wait up for him, so serious is his misdemeanour, and walks into a wall of negativity. "Jeez, not again!" he thinks to himself "What now?" Mum tells him what has transpired. "Geoffrey, come here! Now you listen to me, young man, when are you going to stop making work for your mother? Because that is all you do, make work for me and your mother, now get out of my sight!" Dad goes to the sideboard and pours himself some gin.

At this point in our story, we must remember that Geoffrey's frontal cortex is not yet online. He doesn't yet have the capacity to reason – and so he believes that he has done a bad thing and is a bad person. He doesn't even know when he is being bad. Poor little lad has neither the power nor the intellectual equipment to say something like: "Excuse me Mother! Excuse me Father, but I think you will find that I was behaving in an age-appropriate manner and that, in reality, you are projecting your own hurt and anxiety onto me. Now, I shall go to my room and read for a while and let you think about this. When I come down I shall expect us all to sit down and discuss."

By this we can see that for many people addiction is an adaptation – a survival mechanism. I do believe that some may not have survived if it weren't for the fact that they suffered with addiction. Of course, in this example, it is worth remembering that Geoffrey's parents too will have had their childhood traumas – their parents would have likely experienced some trauma through the First World War, and all the way back to the Crusades. We are part of our collective narratives, and human beings are beset on all sides by grief, fear, anger and pain – to name a few large nouns. When we consider the addicted individual in this new light, we will feel a new kind of sympathy and understanding as we go about family life.

But we still have work to do to understand the terrible nature of family addiction. We must now look very closely at what it means to be a family.

Exercise 2

As you go about your daily routines, begin to pay attention to how often alcohol and drugs get a mention. It may be you are in your car listening to the radio and the presenter is suggesting to some caller that they enjoy a glass or two of something, because that is what they will be doing later. Perhaps a work colleague is boasting about how wasted they were at the weekend. You might be watching an "edgy" BBC crime drama that is depicting people smoking cannabis or taking cocaine in a way that covertly seems to normalise it. Just begin to develop a kind of "Spider Sense" for the normalisation of drugs and alcohol. You might be surprised or perhaps even shocked. Please don't misunderstand me here. I am not anti-alcohol or even anti-drugs, I believe people can do what they wish as long as no harm is done to others, but the normalisation of powerful psychotropic toxins is at best irresponsible and at worst dangerous.

Dark Sun:

A New Approach to Families and Addiction

CHAPTER THREE:

WHAT IS A FAMILY?

It is astonishing and even terrifying that one can go on for years living with a false picture of oneself; and even with a wish to know, to have no real picture of how one manifests oneself. How can the 'dead' know, when even those who are beginning to wake from sleep find it so difficult?"

~ C.S. Nott 'Teachings Of Gurdjieff: A Pupil's Journal'

Mullah Nasruddin, may the sun never go down on his illustrious name, was on a pilgrimage. He had walked for many miles along a desert road and now, at evening, he was exhausted, hungry and very thirsty. Imagine his joy at arriving at a large and opulent caravanserai where there was food and drink a plenty. At last replete, the good Mullah makes his weary way to the sleeping tent. To his horror, the tent is full with other snoring and coughing pilgrims and there is but one bed space left. The Mullah is so tired that he reluctantly makes his way to the last cot and lies down, but sleep evades him. He cannot get away from the fear that if he falls asleep among all these people, he will not remember who he is when he wakes up. So he tosses and turns and mutters and mumbles until a young fellow in the cot next door, having worked out the Mullah's plight, says to him "Don't worry Mullah, I have a solution for your dilemma. Take this pumpkin, yours for only 100 dinari, and with this ribbon, 20 dinari, tie it to your leg. When you awake, you will know who you are by the pumpkin tied to your leg. Delighted, the Mullah handed over the cash, tied the pumpkin to his leg and drifted into a deep and peaceful sleep. During the night, the young scoundrel got up, undid the pumpkin and tied it firmly to the leg of a man in the cot opposite to the Mullah. Chuckling to himself, he made his way out of the sleeping tent. In the morning, Nasruddin awoke and happily looked down at his leg expecting to find the pumpkin. It wasn't there! In a panic he leapt up and ran over to the man opposite. "Wake up!" cried the Mullah "You have a pumpkin tied to your leg and that means you must be me and if you are me who on earth am I?"

Case History 3

Families are founded on belief but such a foundation may be unstable or even unreal. Please excuse me while I refer you to that eminently pragmatic moment in the Gospel According to Matthew – Chapter VII, verses 24-27 – sometimes known as the Wise and Foolish Builders:

Therefore whosoever heareth these sayings of mine, and doeth them, I will liken him unto a wise man, which built his house upon a rock: and the rain descended, and the floods came, and the winds blew, and beat upon that house; and it fell not: for it was founded upon a rock. And every one that heareth these sayings of mine, and doeth them not, shall be likened unto a foolish man, which built his house upon the sand: and the rain descended, and the floods came, and the winds blew, and beat upon that house; and it fell: and great was the fall of it.

The Canons considered themselves a financial family, and an important molecule in the banking organs of this country. Father worked in the City. His father had done the same and so on back through the generations into the smogs of banking history. Mrs. Canon was an expert on schools and universities and so even before Henry Canon had been born his education and eventual initiation into the arcane world of finance had been meticulously calculated with the skill of an 18ᵗʰ century naval captain. Thus Henry, after some preliminary time at Papplewick or some other suitable boarding prep school, would attend Eton and then Oxford. If he were to become a Member of Parliament (Conservative, naturally) on this journey – well, that was all to the good.

The only fly in Mrs Canon's micromanaged ointment was that Henry had other ideas. He dropped out of Eton, was sent to Stowe where he failed his A-Levels with alacrity. Now he was adrift, living at home with a serious cannabis and online gaming addiction. It is my belief that at this point, Henry had simply given up.

The Canons made an appointment to see me. The pricking sensation in my thumbs told me I had a struggle ahead.

They wanted, or rather required, me to persuade Henry to submit to a summer of intense private tutoring and the retaking of his A levels in the hope that some half-decent university would accept him.

After listening to them for a while, I ventured a few questions.

"How old is Henry?"

"He is 19."

"19 in June."

The first from Mr Canon and the correction from Mrs.

"Do we know what Henry would wish for his life?"

"Yes, he has some notion of being a musician!"

"Oh, that's interesting. Can he play an instrument?"

"Yes, he is a very good pianist, even makes up his own tunes. At prep school they said he had a talent."

"So what happened?"

Mr Canon was very definite in his reply.

"As I'm sure you must realise, there's no money in playing the piano and we are a solid banking family. If he could just get the necessary qualifications, he could look forward to a very successful career in the City. I have influence and could introduce him to all sorts of useful people."

I was tempted to ask if that was what Henry wanted, but didn't. Instead I agreed to see Henry for an assessment.

Henry was a sweet-natured boy, quiet and respectful with none of the surly teenage energy I have come to expect in these sessions. He even addressed me as "Sir". We talked about his music and his playing, how he really enjoyed Chopin. This really surprised me. If he was familiar with Chopin, then he must have skill. But something about Henry worried me and worried me enough to recommend a psychiatric assessment. Underneath the quiet and polite surface, there was a sense of hopelessness, almost despair that was a serious cause for concern. Henry agreed to the assessment, provided his father was in agreement. I pointed out that Henry was 19 and did not need his parent's consent, but Henry insisted.

A week later, I met with the parents again. They were not keen on my idea. Instead, they were concerned it would appear on his medical records and interfere with his chances of a decent job – that same job that his father was sure would solve everything. Even though I knew it was practically hopeless, I did my best to fight Henry's corner. He clearly had talent, he loved music and was knowledgeable in a number of areas that had convinced me that he could think deeply. It was all to no avail. In the end, I looked Mr Canon in the eye and asked: "Mr Canon, have you ever even met your son?"

Mr Canon was startled for a moment, then said "I think we're done here." And left. I had failed.

Just over a year later, I learned through the grapevine that Henry had taken his own life.

DEFINING FAMILY

Consider this. If you were to meet the members of your family at a dinner party or some other social occasion, how inclined would you be to see them again, if, let's say, you'd never met them before and they are not, for the purposes of this exercise, your family? What makes one feel obliged to connect with family? Where does that obligation arise? Yes, we can use vague platitudes about blood and water and so forth – but, quite frankly, the bonds of common purpose are stronger than those of family.

Trying to define "family" is intrinsically problematic, since there is no "objective unit of analysis". Very often too, there is also a historical "reference person" around which a set of values and beliefs collect. "We are descended from Robert the Bruce" – or "Your great great grandfather invented lard." And so on. Interestingly, the Middle English sense of the word family referred to all the descendants of a common ancestor. The word comes from the Latin *familia* meaning a household servant or the retinue of a nobleman, and derives from *familius*, meaning *servant*. Like so much of value, this notion of serving something higher or from the past is out of step with modern thinking, but it gives a fascinating insight into the dynamics of a family. What is being served and why? What might the "conditions of belonging" – and remember these might be covert or overt – to a particular family be? In fact, if we can look at families through the different lens of an inherited set of principles which we are somehow expected to serve, then we will reach some surprising conclusions about who we are and how we might best live our lives. Such an approach may also lead us to realise what a valuable rebellion can sometimes look like.

A family can be seen as the means by which some historical quintessence is preserved and passed down through the ages, and it is this notion which children are usually expected to serve. If this is the case, then it can cause harm to the individual, since they are subservient to the intrinsic provenance of that particular family. Typically, this establishes a set of conditions which have to be met if one is to be a part of the family: a pattern of conformism is set in motion. We have to fit in and fitting in is categorically not the same as belonging: fitting in is conditional, whereas belonging is unconditional. We come into the world full of expectations secondary to who we might really be deep down. My experience is that this misunderstanding is very often at the centre of the addiction predicament, and of course, it can play out in multiple ways in the family's reaction to the presence of addiction in the household.

As ever, this can manifest subtly, and so it can help to have some examples which are somewhat easier to spot. In Britain, the class system is perhaps the most obvious example of inherited ideas which can spoil an individual's sense of the essential elasticity of life: this country is liberally stocked with the scions of the wealthy who couldn't find their own path because of the confusion of being born into some supposedly exalted station in life. Conversely, many people think that they are born into a lowdown position in society and so develop imposter syndrome, or some crippling lack of self-confidence just because of these social structures. Professions can also exert a strong pull on individuals within families. Imagine a family today. Father is a QC. His father was a judge as was his grandfather and so on right back to *Lampleigh vs Brathewait* in 1615. Mother is a matriarch of this legal dynasty and so, when father is out being a QC she is organising the children's education, social life and anything else that she can control to make sure they can perpetuate the dynasty. Schools, universities, and even friends are chosen in this powerful dynastic light. In families like this, in my experience, despite the fact that the world has far more people who aren't lawyers in it than it has lawyers, the news that the first-born son wants to run his own card business, or drive a bus, or even be an accountant, may cause considerable dismay across the family system. Would we be surprised if that son, once he gets forced into the law, begins to drink a little to numb the sense that he's not doing what he's supposed to do with his life at the crucial level of his individual self?

Or perhaps Father is a miner. His father was also a miner and so on back to the beginnings of the Industrial Revolution. The family live in a mining community with schools, activities, literature and even songs organised around the mining culture. And yet in the next generation his child suddenly aspires to university! Again, there is dismay and again we can see how this dismay can easily lead to a deep-seated unease in the child which may manifest eventually as addiction.

These examples are intentionally clear, but it's worth remembering that the weight of dynasty bears down on us all and often in very subtle ways. In the vast majority of cases it informs our beliefs, thinking, and behaviour and even our emotional engagement with the world. This means that limitations are placed on all of us without realising it. Some may live their whole lives blissfully unaware that they were ever handed this script at all. Others may be beset with a nagging sense that something isn't quite right. A very few awaken to this reality and begin to forge a true identity; interestingly, I think it is this which addicts are sometimes trying to do, though they have chosen a particularly dangerous way of doing so.

But once we accept this new understanding of family, the question then arises: "Well then, who am I in all this?". This is an excellent question and one really can't ask this of oneself enough.

SURVIVAL LOGIC

But instead of asking ourselves this question, many prefer to enter into the condition which I call survival logic.

What do I mean by this? It is fear-based logic based on a perceived belief that the environment is hostile, one needs to survive at all costs and, above all, that the biggest danger is change. Indeed this is a frequent characteristic in most families. It is the reason why many children return to live after university near to where their parents live, and why many people live such similar lives: *Whatever happens, change must be avoided*. This attitude breeds a kind of togetherness based on fear and not on love. If we look closely at this attitude it has nothing to do with the well-being of the individual; instead it is about the perceived survival of the herd. In fact, if necessary, the individual will be sacrificed for the supposed safety of the herd. Togetherness of this kind stifles, homogenises and stultifies. 'I' becomes 'We' and everybody ceases to think, or live and love, independently. This is pernicious and leads to unhappy lives.

On the other hand, the family is a vital component of human life, and needs to be made healthy. We all need the collective connection and safety of family: it is essential for the development of an individual. The care, nurturing and security the system brings is one of the great qualities of the human race. The word "kind" is related to the word "kin": when we speak of being kind to animals, we are saying they should be treated as family. This fact alone is liberating: we do not need to be related by blood for kindness to happen. It has been truthfully observed that a village is necessary to bring up children and that common cause is stronger than blood. This healthy form of togetherness is founded in love and in respect for the uniqueness of the individual. A system based on loving togetherness will produce a nurturing ecology which embraces difference and prepares the individual for a successful entry into adulthood and a functional separation.

The forces of separation in a family were once signposted by various rites of passage. Sadly, in today's beige gruel of a world these have vanished to a large extent and the young adult is left floundering between a need to grow up and leave and an overwhelming sense of not being equipped to survive in the world as it is. All too often, young people see adulthood appearing over the horizon and at a deep level fear that there is no place for them there. They then resort to camouflage, or vanish into rebellion, or try out a kind of static perfectionism: in short they have chosen survival logic, and they have become lost children. Sadly, the world is full of such people.

Fairy tales will often allude to these crossing points or transitions when the hero or heroine would 'set out to seek their fortune'. There is little in today's world that validates the experience of uncertainty and discomfort that typifies the "betwixt and between" world of the young modern adult. The transition into adulthood is very fragile and very important: it could even be viewed as a second birth whereby the child is helped and encouraged into full womanhood or manhood. Where are the 'elders' to facilitate this? Where are the rituals? One could say that the Gap Year traveller is undergoing a rite of passage, or a young adult joining the armed forces, or going to university and yes, these all have the externals of a rite of passage but there is rarely a guide or mentor to support the inwardness of such journeys. What is missing in the modern world are the tribal elders, wise ones tasked with bringing the child into internal adulthood.

THE GOVERNMENT OF THE FAMILY

It is helpful to think of the family as a system, a collection of parts trying to become a whole. This whole needs a governor, a word derived from the Latin, *gubenare*, to steer and the Greek, *kubernan*, to drive, pilot or be a steersman. It's interesting to note that the word cybernetic has the same root: oarsman or that which steers.

Each family has a different oarsman, and it is important to realise that this needn't necessarily be a person – a patriarch or matriarch. More often it is a principle, a set of beliefs, a heritage, or some distant icon. In this sense, a family is very much like a nation: it is likely that one member of the family seeks to embody these principles, and therefore carries them forwards to the next generation. Of course, very often the situation is complicated by marriage, whereby we see the collision of two powerful reference histories. This can be very problematic: perhaps a so-called "commoner" might marry into royalty, or a non-Catholic marrying into a Catholic family system. But even these examples are simplifications. In reality what happens is that multiple streams of provenance cascade down through the ages, out of the obscurity of history: born into a strange world, we mechanically sacrifice ourselves to these concepts, almost always with negative results, including, but not confined to, addictive behaviours.

Two powerful forces at play within the family system are 'togetherness' and 'separateness'. As a family changes, one might observe these forces in action. Let's say a family consists of wife, husband and two young children. It is likely that much in these first stages is done as a unit: the needs of the young ones acting as a governor to the system. As the children grow older, the forces of separation begin to come into play – the children want their own rooms, have different friends and so forth. Also the parents feel somewhat released to pursue individual interests. The forces of separation gradually strengthen until the offspring eventually leave home. Let's consider an example from the animal kingdom. The fulmar is a seabird that nests on the high cliffs of North West Scotland. They mate for life and mostly return to the same nest every season. They are doting and protective parents virtually sacrificing themselves to their chicks' well-being until it is time for the chicks to leave the nest. But then, all love and care cast aside, the parent birds pick the chicks up in their beaks and throw them off the cliff. If the chick cannot fly, well, that is no longer the concern of the parent.

Sometimes the system exhibits a certain degree of balance, meaning that it is able to function in a broadly healthy manner. Where these forces are out of balance, the system will swiftly become unhealthy and tend towards pathology: this might manifest as enmeshment, fusion, isolation or alienation, depending on the nature of that imbalance. Enmeshment is a manifestation of an excess of the force of togetherness. The umbilical cord has not been cut: indeed any nourishment now tends to flow backwards, from child to parent. Abandonment, where the needs of the child are subsumed to the needs of the parent leading to neglect, is an excess of separateness. If there is addiction arisen in a family system, these forces are very likely to be pathologically out of balance.

Parenting styles often amount to a form of imitation and may even be based on superstition and hearsay; more importantly still, they are often more centred in the parents' wishes for themselves than in the well-being of the children.

So if families exist not just in space, but also in time, who or what should govern the family? The answer is that we need to be governed by an awareness of this reality. This trans-generational stream is sadly ignored in the treatment of addiction, especially when academic research wants to push the illness towards a brain disease with powerful genetic components. Addicted people have a good reason to use and that reason is that they are in great pain, and the addictive process is a means of trying to survive. Often, I have spoken with one time addicted souls who are now in what is called recovery who have stated clearly that their addiction saved their lives: in effect it was either heroin/ alcohol/ gambling – or it was suicide.

But if we make a leap in our understanding and accept this complex web of inherited ideas, then it might be we can begin to understand better what it means to be in a family. In my experience, this understanding will tend to go hand in hand with a deeper sense of the addict's behaviour, and the reasons for it.

THE BIG BAG OF STUFF

If addiction is a misguided yet not entirely irrational response to hurt – a rational reaction to a wounding of some sort – then when and by whom were these wounds inflicted? That's a difficult question.

The answer has to do with history. In my experience, families act out the dramas of the past, both the recent and the not-so-recent: the range of our influences is far larger than we might imagine as we go about our quotidian lives. To take today as an example, we are still living in the shadow of two incomprehensible World Wars, one of which ended with the creation and using of the atomic bomb: ever since, we have known that humanity has the means to exterminate itself in a matter of moments. As a result of our propensity for conflict, all of the human race is suffering with trauma and the toxic beliefs and behaviours that accompany this. This, of course, plays itself out at the level of nations – but also at the level of smaller units like towns, villages, streets, and households.

In families then, we are implicated in a highly complex and largely unconscious web of beliefs, attitudes and worldviews. Consider, for example, what it means when someone is attached, or attaches themselves, to the term "working class". By this attachment, the individual is arrogating to themselves a set of values and beliefs that in terms of the individuals real self, may have no objective reality. Alongside these beliefs and values will come certain feelings and ways of thinking, none of which are necessarily the real perspectives of the person. Whilst working with developmental trauma, I have often witnessed a temporary state of disorientation in a client when they realise at a deep level that a great deal of what they believed to be their own personality and even self was in fact made up of characteristics, values, beliefs, attitudes and even feelings that had been interjected into them by the family and social system and that, in reality, had no bearing upon the person's real self.

When any soul enters into planetary existence they are handed, by the family and the society at large, a big bag of *stuff*.

This stuff has many different qualities. Some of it is actually useful; some of it might resemble the things you find in the back of the fridge when you return from a long holiday. But there are certain things which seem to be the case always: the stuff seems to be **right**, it seems to be **important** and it seems to be **valuable**.

These appearances are very strong, but tend to be false. But their potency is the reason why, as soon as the new human is old enough to begin rummaging around in the bag, the stuff starts to take over their life. It tells them how and what to think, how to feel, how to believe and even who they are. The bag of stuff becomes the person, or rather, the person climbs into the bag of stuff and vanishes. So then, when two people meet later on in life and begin to form a relationship, they start to rummage around in the bags of stuff and bring out exhibits and bits and bobs to define every situation. This invariably leads to difficulties. This is my stuff and my stuff is right! How can your stuff be both different to my stuff and be right? That is not possible, my stuff is the objective truth! You can see from this how wars begin. It is stuff that cause wars. Except as paradigms, there are no such things as classes, middle, working or otherwise, or religions, or political leanings, or any of the other things in the big bag of stuff to which we became so unconsciously and pathologically attached to the extent that we will fight to the death over something that actually has no meaningful reality.

External events will seep into family culture and become part of the individual member's adapted self. As before, when it comes to thinking about how this happens, it is helpful to take a vivid example, while realising that in most families a similar process may be taking place in a multitude of subtle, and therefore, well-hidden ways. Let's consider the example of the family icon – a grandparent or great-grandparent who did something extraordinary in the Second World War and who is now revered and held up as an example to all. Perhaps the grandfather was a spitfire pilot, shot down in the Battle of Britain. Perhaps the great-grandmother escaped from the Nazi death camps, walked across Europe and set herself up in England. Perhaps you, or someone else in your family, is named after one of these heroes. Whatever the provenance and circumstance – and no matter how brave and enterprising the icon may have been – their huge shadowy presence in the family history will have considerable impact upon their descendants' self-esteem. Let us now consider a more subtle transgenerational trauma. Imagine a couple in the early fifties. They have been through World War Two and the Great Slump before it. They meet and fall in love and vow to put all that trauma behind; to shut the door on it forever. To effect this, they create what they imagine to be the perfect family. They buy a small farm, have goats, chickens, puppies and kittens and a washing-line. Their three children have what looks like an idyllic childhood with mummy smiling constantly and daddy smoking his pipe and reading Rupert Bear at bedtime. The children grow up believing they have had a perfect childhood and wonder why at age 45 they hit a wall of anxiety and depression when their own children descend into drinking and drug use. They simply do not understand that, with the best will in the world, they were coerced into their parents' vision of perfection and complicit in their parents' denial about the original need to create such a household. All along there was something unexamined about the idyll – a gap. But there was no darkness – there were no shadows visible. Trauma can lie dormant like this, and then suddenly spring up. There is no blame attached to any of this; what matters is to observe that such impacts do occur – and in fact, are occurring across our troubled planet day in day out. I speak here, like everybody else, from personal experience: I was brought up by traumatised parents, who had lived through terrible times and had received no help at all with their trauma. I was "educated" by a cohort of angry, brutalised and frightened men who had also been traumatised. So where does this trauma go? It is poured into the upcoming generation and left with them for them to deal with as best they can. This is why we need to break that cycle. How do we do that? We must start to question some of the founding principles of one's own family – those people and events held up as making *this* family what it is. We shall learn much by looking at this very closely.

CLOCKWORK FAMILIES

Given the above, one might wonder how, when two people from different families meet and get married, the process of negotiating realities can be started? It is indeed a complicated process which people usually have no stars to navigate by and so they muddle through.

The family is a complex system or ecosystem of relationships wherein each member sees a different family. The mother might come from a banking dynasty who are dyed-in-the-wool Tory; the father might come from a family of engineers who have tended to vote Labour. Immediately we have a recipe for a misfiring system, where what is essential is up for grabs. If that system is full of love, it can of course be a rich inheritance where the offspring have a broad worldview, which perhaps can tee them up well for understanding different aspects of life, and reconciling paradox. But often confusion will predominate even though everybody is doing their best. In such families, the script will be unclear, and the big bag of stuff full of contradictions. Accordingly, it might be we enter a hall of mirrors, where we are baffled by our lives. But one way or another this system, whether contradictory or clear, will end up making covert (and overt) demands on the individual members.

Many therefore deploy camouflage to avoid the difficulty and pain of the real self being seen. Sometimes, the camouflage is addiction.

Usually within the imperious nature of the demands is disagreement about their precise nature leading to confusion and disharmony. Ask different siblings to describe, say, their father and you will get very different responses. Accordingly, each individual of a family will see the family entity quite differently – even though the inherited principles of that family are making similarly strict demands on everyone. One sibling, for example may love their father as a kind and comforting presence whereas another may see him as weak and pathetic, or as an ogre of discipline. In fact it turns out that there are as many families as there are individual members.

Some of this may come as surprising or even distressing news. But this information turns out to be important when it comes to tackling addiction. Family members are interdependent, or co-dependent: they tend to inhabit a pathological system. This might be a sub-optimal state of affairs but it also constitutes a sort of opportunity: the thoughts, feelings and behaviours of one member will greatly affect another; thus if one member changes, the other members will feel this change and possibly change in response. As we saw in the first chapter, by taking control of your own life, it is therefore possible to alter the nature of the whole system, including a system in which addiction has taken control. Of course, especially initially, an addict will resist that change – but this book is written in the belief that by committing to a complete overhaul of one's own life, one can genuinely alter the status quo in whatever struggling family you might be a member of.

Picture a clock; an old clockwork clock with cogs and wheels and springs. The functioning of each cog or wheel is entirely dependent on the others, so if one element changes, the other elements either change reciprocally or powerfully resist the change. Imagine a family. For generations this family has been what is called "working class". One of the recent family members is gifted and wins a scholarship to a red brick university. Whereas this family has always worked locally doing manual work, perhaps in local factories or agriculture, this member now has the opportunity to change. The system may well resist this change and employ tactics of shame, which is inherent in the system anyway, and anxiety.

Families are like clocks; they operate by systemic feeling. Anxiety, shame and anger are examples of negative system feelings. Hope, joy and love are positive examples. These system feelings are trans-generational in that they move through the family timeline with each generation. If parents are anxious, they will give the child the impression that something is wrong and will likely adapt by becoming the thing that is wrong! If a child is seen by the parents as having low self-esteem, their attempts to affirm and compensate are likely to render the child dependent on external validation. If a young child is treated as an adult and given too much choice, say over meals, bedtimes and so on, the child will take on an inappropriate sense of responsibility and become very anxious and concerned with getting it right. Children may become as sensitive to the needs and wants of the parents as the parents are to the child's.

But we need to get used to seeing this reality as an opportunity for beneficial change, by using to our advantage. If we inhabit an interconnected clockwork family – as we all do – then any love which we can pour into that system will have a consequence elsewhere. When we consider love, we must be very careful not to confuse it with some of the tropes I outlined in the first Chapter: thinking we know better; hand-holding and molly-cuddling; foisting our own preferences onto the loved one – these are all behaviours which we might confuse with love, but which must be strenuously avoided. I shall be returning to these themes in my final chapter.

THE SCAPEGOAT-CARETAKER DYNAMIC

But before we consider what it might be to wake up, we have to realise that we are asleep. Most families are in this condition.

That's because the fundamental characteristic of an intricate emotional arrangement like the family is that people tend to pressure one another into thinking and acting alike, particularly when anxiety escalates. This promotes a sense of togetherness and well-being, but it also instigates a powerful set of denial mechanisms. Denial is ubiquitous in all families. It is the comfortable sleep state that prevents us going quite mad and allows us to dream lovely dreams of respectability and decency. Denial is difficult to address because the person in denial cannot, or will not, see past the walls of denial. It is easy to spot in the identified addict, but not so apparent in the addicted family system.

So how does this denial manifest? In my experience, it goes like this. An important aspect of the undercover life of a family (and indeed of any system) is the assigning and taking up of roles. It's very necessary to be aware that every stick has two ends, and that a role is both assigned and accepted: there is reciprocity in this process. It is useful here to have a brief discussion of the different roles and the uses to which they are put by the family system, although the outline below is by no means exhaustive.

When addiction arises in the family, the roles become more pronounced, more rigid and much more difficult to detach from – and that happens to be the case even after the addiction is no longer active.

Often, the identified addict is handed and steps into the role of Scapegoat. Wikipedia has this to say about scapegoats. "The scapegoat was a goat that was designated (Hebrew: לַעֲזָאזֵל) la-'aza'zeyl;" for absolute removal" (for symbolic removal of the people's sins with the literal removal of the goat), and outcast in the desert as part of the ceremonies of the Day of Atonement, that began during the Exodus with the original Tabernacle and continued through the times of the temples in Jerusalem." Other online sources state that the scapegoat is one who is blamed for something or things that others have done.

All of this gets us into the right ballpark – but none of it is quite right. The scapegoat does not accept blame, rather the scapegoat becomes a *container* for whatever is awry in the family system. This is different to simply being blamed. The scapegoat's role is rather similar to that of the ancient idea of the 'sin-eater', which arises in ancient British cultures, especially in Welsh culture. The idea is that the 'sin-eater', by eating a ritual meal takes on and carries the sins of the people whose sins they have eaten. Once you start to consider this concept, you will see that society is full of necessary containers. For example, one major function of a psychiatric hospital is to act as a container for society's fear of madness; the church acts a container for the fear of death and so on. Below the surface, in the deep undercurrents of the collective unconscious there are many scapegoats or containers. In the addicted family system, the scapegoat becomes an attractor for all the actual and potential "sins" of that system and allows the other members to remain unsullied. "Sarah is really struggling at university!". "Yes I know, but she must be so worried about her brother!": "Freddie and Hugo are always arguing and fighting, they used to be so close!" "I put it down to their father's alcoholism" and so on and so. The scapegoat serves everyone and allows everyone to avoid themselves and remain in denial. The whole process of scapegoating and being scapegoated is part of our joint sleep.

Powerfully associated with this idea of the Scapegoat is the role of Caretaker. The Scapegoat-Caretaker dynamic becomes the central sun around which every other part of the system must orbit. As we glimpsed in Chapter One, the Caretaker believes absolutely that they can "fix" the scapegoat; that they know the scapegoat better than anyone else possibly can and as such "understand" better than anyone else can, even experienced professionals. The Caretaker becomes so identified with their role that they get completely lost within it and their entire sense of self becomes entirely defined by this role. It is the Caretaker who is there at 4am when the scapegoat blunders in, completely drunk. It is the Caretaker who cleans them up and puts them to bed. It is the Caretaker who phones the scapegoat's work the next morning with an excuse for them. The Caretaker's well-being is absolutely dependent on the Scapegoat. If the Scapegoat is happy, the Caretaker is happy. But if the Scapegoat is anxious or angry, it must be because of the Caretaker and the Caretaker cannot rest until they have "fixed" the situation. This dynamic is very dangerous for all concerned and in many instances can prove fatal, especially for the addict.

We spoke earlier about the Big Bag of Stuff and it needs to be understood that these roles coalesce around the existence of this: the Scapegoat is in a flawed opposition to the Big Bag of Stuff, and wants to make his own life, but has no inclination how to do it. The Caretaker exists solely in relation to the Scapegoat. But usually there will be someone who seeks to uphold the family provenance and keep the Big Bag of Stuff in tact to hand onto the next generation. This is the Hero: in a family of engineers, he will seek to be the person to fix HS2. If it is a religious family the Hero will likely enter the priesthood. If the family is working class, they will become a Labour councillor. It is the Hero's job to ensure the social acceptability of the dynasty and to develop and enhance its image in the world. Sadly, this quest is an entirely bogus one and the Hero is often avoidant, and resentful at the fact that he could not become a florist.

These roles are what might be termed "inner adult" roles. That's not to say that children don't take them on: in fact, one particularly painful circumstance is when a child is coerced into becoming a parent's caretaker and thereby sacrifices their childhood. Similarly the child might be forced into becoming the Hero. However, these examples, though I have seen them both many times, are relatively rare.

INNER CHILD ROLES

More common are what might be called "inner child" roles. These are the Mascot and the Clown. The task of these roles is to lessen tension and divert conflict. As such, children co-opted into these roles have very sensitive *solar plexi* and can feel a fight long, long before anyone else. The Mascot will usually use a performance to defuse the situation whereas the clown will use humour. Faced with the possible outbreak of intra-family hostilities, the Mascot may be asked to sing or play some sort of instrument whereas the clown will do or say something humorous that will allow the family to re-focus away from the confrontation and onto the Mascot or Scapegoat.

Christmas lunch is rich with opportunities to observe roles. Relatives from far and wide are invited to this ordeal and perfection is demanded in every aspect. Stephen the Hero is coming from Mars, and several aunts whom no-one knew about are threatening to descend also. Lunch is under way, Stephen is regaling everyone with tales of the Red Planet, Tim the Scapegoat is drunk and obnoxious while Mother is doing her best to manage him. War between Stephen and Tim is looming, Clarissa has slipped away to her bedroom, unnoticed until mother asks her to fetch the custard. Everyone has a knotted stomach, everyone is smiling valiantly. Just before the tension between Stephen and Tim turns into violence, Mother says to her other son, much younger, 'Oh I know, Charlie why don't you get your guitar and play that song you are learning for everyone?' This is the Mascot role, the mascot's job is to perform and to bypass any conflict. The Clown has a similar role except they will use humour and crack a joke, or fart spectacularly or pour custard over the nearest aunt. So often I come across these roles in group therapy where invariably and pre-consciously the family dynamic of each group member will present itself. The group may be getting emotional and quite intense: the Clown, unable to manage this intensity will crack a joke or make a funny remark. Equally, the Mascot might set off on a long story about when they met Sting in a bar in Mumbai and divert in that way.

Another common inner child role is the Lost Child. The Lost Child copes with the toxic family undertow by becoming invisible: they quite simply vanish. They learn to survive and often start to read at an early age. This allows them to escape to their room, where they have biscuits and supplies under the bed, and avoid the rest of the family. This often is passed over with a dialogue like this:

"Where is Clarissa?"

"Oh she's in her room reading the book you gave her. She is such a clever little thing. She could read almost before she could walk!"

One way or another, lost children vanish. Sometimes they actually vanish and leave home very early – but more often they vanish emotionally and become so well-behaved that no-one notices them: "Oh Jeremy is such a good boy, he's *never* any trouble at all!"

There is nothing intrinsically wrong or bad about these roles; roles are an essential and useful part of everyday life. In my work, I am often called upon to play a role of one sort or another, and this is part of the skill of the job. The difficulties arise when we become unconsciously over identified with a particular role and come to believe that the role is in fact who we are. This is a good example of ego governing our lives. Ego is a useful servant but a bad master. In the addicted family system, over-identification with the above roles is pretty much the norm. It is not only the person carrying the role that becomes over-identified but also the whole family and thus we get seemingly innocent asides such as, "Oh Billy, he's the troublemaker!" or "Jill is always such a good girl." This creates and perpetuates a rigid and toxic dynamic wherein no one member may relinquish their assigned role. Instead, everyone clings to their own and everyone else's role as if to a life-saving log in a deluge.

I have seen these sorts of processes amount to counter-recovery. The power of identification may even drag the identified addict back into an old and obsolete role if the family dynamic remains unchanged. It may even be that this circumstance triggers a relapse. When, as so often is the case, a family member, new to a support group, asks how they can help and support their loved one's recovery, they are often taken aback when I respond with: "Begin to recognise your own part in the pathology and become willing to deal with it." This is not what the average family member wants to hear and all the more so as they have been leaning heavily on the other's addiction as an alibi for not having to change.

One cannot repeat this enough: addiction is a family illness. Simply assigning the whole kit and caboodle of pathology to one family member and expecting everything to work out is genuinely crazy.

Exercise 3

You may want to set aside a little more time for this exercise in family constellations. First of all, find some small objects such as pebbles, marbles, small tiles or anything that you can use to represent members of your family. Take some time to relax and slow down your thinking: this is not an intellectual exercise. Now on a table or a tray or on the floor, pick one of the chosen objects to represent yourself. Without over-thinking, place it in a position that you feel represents where you are now. Don't agonise over this: if you can't decide, just place it somewhere central. Now, think of another member of your family: perhaps a parent or a spouse. Use the space around your object to describe the relationship. Perhaps you feel close to this person, then place them close and so on. Don't be afraid to get creative with this process. You might decide that one aspect of a chosen object is their face and you might place them "facing" away from you and so on. Do this for as many members of your family and extended family as you like. Include grandparents, pets, and even relatives long dead that you have never met but you still feel have an influence. Perhaps your great-great-grandfather did something dreadful, or heroic and that stream still flows through the system dynamic. When you feel you have completed this part, spend some time reflecting upon your constellation, paying particular attention to how you are feeling about certain relationships.

If you have the inclination, ask yourself some questions about your place in the system. When you are done, rearrange the objects in a way that you would like. Perhaps you wish to feel closer to your sister, or wish that your father would turn towards you. Use your objects to make that happen and again pay close attention to any feelings that may arise. If you are very diligent, you might like to write something about this experience.

Dark Sun:

A New Approach to Families and Addiction

PART TWO: THE JOURNEY HOME

Dark Sun:

A New Approach to Families and Addiction

CHAPTER 4

THE NEED FOR CHANGE

In the beginning there was nothing. And God said, "Let there be Light!" there was still nothing, but now you could see it.

Groucho Marx

Nasrudin was walking along a lonely road one moonlit night when he heard a snore, somewhere, it seemed, underfoot. Suddenly he was afraid, and was about to run when he tripped over a dervish lying in a cell which he had dug for himself, partly underground. 'Who are you?' stammered the Mulla. 'I am a dervish, and this is my contemplation-place.' 'You will have to let me share it. Your snore frightened me out of my wits, and I cannot go any further tonight.' 'Take the other end of this blanket, then,' said the dervish without enthusiasm, 'and lie down here. Please be quiet, because I am keeping a vigil. It is a part of a complicated series of exercises. Tomorrow I must change the pattern, and I cannot stand interruption.' Nasrudin fell asleep for a time. Then he woke up, very thirsty. 'I am thirsty,' he told the dervish. 'Then go back down the road, where there is a stream.' 'No, I am still afraid.' 'I shall go for you, then,' said the dervish. After all, to provide water is a sacred obligation in the East. 'No - don't go. I shall be afraid all by myself.' 'Take this knife to defend yourself with,' said the dervish. While he was away, Nasrudin frightened himself still more, working himself up into a lather of anxiety, which he tried to counter by imagining how he would attack any fiend who threatened him. Presently the dervish returned. 'Keep your distance, or I'll kill you!' said Nasrudin, 'But I am the dervish,' said the dervish. 'I don't care who you are – you may be a fiend in disguise. Besides, you have your head and eyebrows shaved!' The dervishes of that Order shave the head and eyebrows. 'But I have come to bring you water! Don't you remember – you are thirsty!' 'Don't try to ingratiate yourself with me, Fiend!' 'But that is my cell you are occupying!' 'That's hard luck for you, isn't it? You'll just have to find another one.' 'I suppose so,' said the dervish, 'but I am sure I don't know what to make of all this.' 'I can tell you one thing,' said Nasrudin, 'and that is that fear is multi-directional.' 'It certainly seems to be stronger than thirst, or sanity, or other people's property,' said the dervish. 'And you don't have to have it yourself in order to suffer from it!' said Nasrudin.

Case History 4

Jack's mother came to see me in a state of high anxiety. Jack was twenty years old and had a history of self-harm and a disastrous relationship with food that might be called anorexia, although the reality was more complex. The family had lived with Jack's powerful pathology for several years and had grown terrified of what might become of Jack. This terror had initiated all kinds of behaviours which, on close examination, although in normal terms completely understandable, only made the situation worse. They had often felt compelled to break down the bathroom door when they knew Jack was cutting himself, to find the floor covered in blood and Jack clutching a razor blade. His mother would clean him up, bandage him and if necessary take him to A and E – waiting sometimes for hours while he was examined. On most occasions, although there had appeared to be a lot of bleeding, the self-inflicted wounds were not serious.

Jack's mother did all she could to get him to eat. She cooked and plated all his meals (as instructed by the psychiatrist), she sat with him while he toyed with his food and even tried to spoon-feed him. Meanwhile, as a reaction to Jack, his father had become seriously depressed and had been prescribed powerful medication.

The situation seemed almost beyond help, and as I listened to Jack's mother, I felt the familiar urge to offer practical solutions which is what I tend to do when feeling dejected about the prospects of a patient. I knew I had to change the focus. Jack's parents were desperate and exhausted: they were, I felt, on the edge of collapse. I had no idea whether rehab would work for Jack, but it would certainly give the parents an essential break. After a lot of work, Jack agreed to go to rehab. I worked with the parents to get them to the point at which they were able to say to Jack in effect: "If you don't go, you cannot stay here."

So Jack went into treatment. But, surprisingly, Jack had a girlfriend and this girlfriend didn't like the idea of Jack changing. Unbeknown to the parents, she gave Jack an ultimatum and, just a week after he arrived, Jack called his parents to say he wanted to leave treatment. By some miracle, the parents were able to hold the line and say to Jack that he was free to do whatever he wanted, but that if he left, he could not come home. Jack left anyway and moved in with the girlfriend. Quickly this arrangement disintegrated and the girlfriend ended the relationship. Jack wanted to come home. The parents kept the boundary and said: "No". They were willing however to pay for a room for Jack to live in, but he had to find it for himself.

Jack found a room. He signed up for benefits and lived in that room, keeping himself alive for two years. His parents kept in touch and sometimes visited him, which upset Jack's mother as he rarely washed or changed his clothes and lived in squalor. He was eating enough to stay alive and his self-harming had stopped. Quite suddenly, after two years of seeming hopelessness, Jack turned. He washed and changed his clothes, he found himself a job and began to instigate regular contact with his parents. I have since lost contact with the family, but the last I heard was that Jack was transformed.

He was working, he had gone back to college, had a new girlfriend and was often a welcome addition to family gatherings. Miracles do happen.

ENTER A BEWILDERED PARENT

I am often approached by parents asking me to see their son or their daughter, usually because they are at their wits' end with trying to "fix" their child. I may have been recommended through a friend or another professional, and always they are hopeful and enthusiastic about the solution they are considering.

But, very often, herein lies the first difficulty: the parents have a specific outcome in mind to which they cling. The problem is that the desired outcome may well be rather unrealistic in the light of the background circumstances – and, in any case, we can never own outcomes. Let's say their son, who is 23 , has dropped out of university and is drifting with no particular aim or perceived purpose. This is a further unfolding of a process that started much earlier. He may have had disappointing results for his A levels, fallen into bad company and been led astray by others. He was always a kind, considerate and helpful boy, very bright and very good academically and excellent at sports. He was popular. With all this, the parents simply cannot fathom what has happened – how their beloved son has transmogrified into this angry, surly abusive "thing" that they no longer recognise. I often wish I was working in medieval times: if I did, I would be able to tell them: "This is not your child. It is something other, a demonic possession." To my mind, this is a more useful approach than most modern psychological theories; however, it would not sit especially well with the modern psychotherapeutic establishment, and so I often hold my tongue.

But as I have stated earlier, we do need to separate the person from the disease: addiction is not a condition of identity. The sufferer is neither weak nor wicked – they are in the grip of something very powerful over which, without help and information, they have little influence. This disidentification is essential since it separates the possessed from the possessor and gives a clear starting point for recovery.

It also helps to have an answer when a bewildered parent or partner asks me: "What has happened? Where is the person I care about so much?"

I can then answer: "They are being held hostage by a thing, by an It and that It has become their jailer."

Of course, this comfort, as we have seen, can only take us so far. To make matters worse, the It in this equation has convinced the beloved that prison is a safe and attractive place to be, that freedom is very dangerous – and that they will not be able to cope or even survive, outside their jail. The news is in fact even worse than this. Unfortunately, the family member is not able to rescue the loved one from this prison, as the jailer is gifted with extraordinary cunning and is very able to persuade their captive that the family member is actually an enemy – and finally, that it will be extremely painful to awaken from these delusions. Once in a while, a shaft of pure sunshine or moonlight might find its way into the prison cell, momentarily waking the prisoner to their situation. Without genuine help and immediate support, these glimpses are likely to be short and, for that reason, painful. They may be experienced by the family as moments of genuine honesty and remorse before the horrid status quo resumes.

One simple fact that may help with the families' bewilderment and confusion is something we have already looked at: for the addict, their addiction is the Primary Relationship and thus the organising principle of their world. Addiction is king, or rather despot.

This chapter is all about how we wake up to this reality – and what it means to do so. A change – or metanoia if you prefer – of our own attitude is the thing which in the end can navigate us out of our bewilderment.

THE C WORD

As we saw in the last chapter, there are numerous social pressures on the family system: societal expectations, concerns of class, education, income and the like. In the UK, this can raise the question of entitlement. I was struck when, on a recent visit to a treatment centre in Arizona, a colleague of mine, also a visitor, asked the consultant psychiatrist overseeing the treatment: "What is your opinion on the difference between English and American patients?" The answer came back: "Entitlement, the English have a sense of entitlement which makes treatment that bit more difficult." In English family systems there seems to have arisen in recent decades a parental reluctance to let children grow up and leave home.

50 years ago, a 25-year-old would likely have left home and would not involve the parents in their lives except for the sake of protocol and minimal connection. Nowadays, it seems that parents of certain classes are involved to the point of control in their children's lives. This leads to a state of unhealthy enmeshment where the child feels entitled and the parents feel overly responsible. The resulting dynamic contributes to the problems of addiction by drastically lessening – or in some cases, even removing entirely – the impact of the inevitable consequences of addiction. This is a form of covert support of the addiction. Its obverse, where the addict isn't molly-coddled and pandered to in a palatial home, is to simply leave the addict to hit 'rock bottom': by removing the buffering and allowing the full impact of the addiction to be felt, a window of opportunity may open and there is hope for recovery.

When addiction arises in a family system, it destabilises that system and becomes the organising principle. Pathological roles are assigned to everyone, not just the addict. We have already seen how the addiction will inevitably create an unusually high level of intensity and drama. This increase in intensity will hook family members into a kind of dance in which the same inevitable steps are repeated over and over. Strangely, this certainty is comforting in a way as it allows every family member to avoid the C word, which we here introduce into the process: *Change*.

In my experience, humans have an inherent existential dread of things changing. Family systems have endemic beliefs, structures and feelings, and it can be very remarkable how stubborn these notions can be, making change difficult in itself. Just as the identified addict has suffered a loss of control, so the other family members exhibit a reciprocal set of behaviours which add to the intensity of the situation, and to which they are also attached.

Very often what happens is that everybody is attached in ways they may not realise to the addiction itself. Obviously, this is a problem in that it suggests a widespread malady across the whole family system. On the other hand, it means that the family member can always do something to improve the situation – they only need to know how to change.

MEET THE NORMANS

And what would change entail? In this example, I shall attempt a more detailed explanation which is intended to be helpful to those who might think they have no need to change at all. As you read this, put yourself in the shoes of Mr and Mrs Norman and think of all the things they might say to themselves to decide that change is in fact not necessary. Then, see if these alibis in any way apply to your own life. Is there not more we might each do to improve the nature of the family system in which we find ourselves?

Mr and Mrs Norman have been in a stable marriage for thirty years and have raised, or almost raised, three children. Mr Norman never really knew his father – except for a framed photograph and a display of medals on the mantelpiece. His father flew Hurricanes in the Battle of Britain and was shot down over the English Channel. Mr Norman grew up in the shadow of an absent icon, but was never permitted to feel the loss – nor did he ever question this gap in his emotional repertoire. His mother remarried a stern but kind naval officer who believed in a good classical education and the rule of law. Mr Norman went to boarding school at age seven.

Mrs Norman was one of three daughters born to a farming family in Warwickshire. They were wealthy farmers and believed in community and hard work. Her parents had lived through the Depression and the Second World War, and had made a firm decision to put that all behind them, marry and create a perfect life. Mrs Norman describes her childhood as idyllic and denies that her occasional bout of angry depression have anything to do with her past.

Mr Norman works very hard. No-one is quite clear what he does but it attracts a more than substantial salary, with bonuses, and this allows the Normans a more than comfortable lifestyle. The Normans have a beautiful Jacobean house just outside a village somewhere around the Surrey-West Sussex borders. Mr Norman is a very busy man. He stays late in his City office, he is often on business in Dubai, or Boston or Hong Kong. On the occasions that Mr Norman is at home, he likes to spend his time in his shed. He looks at seed catalogues, listens to Radio 4 and frets over the increasing amount of moss in his otherwise immaculate lawn. One of the unacknowledged reasons Mr Norman works so hard and spends so much time in his shed is that he has forgotten how to have, and has become rather awkward at, having a relationship with Mrs Norman.

Mrs Norman loves to be involved in the community. She has a diary full of provisional dates and she can be relied upon to organise any social or community event. Jumble sales, charity concerts, Village celebrations: whatever it is, Mrs Norman can be relied upon to provide and delight. She once even managed to persuade Sir Simon Rattle to conduct the annual village performance of Handel's *Messiah*. She is loved and respected in the community. One of the unacknowledged reasons for Mrs Norman's commitment to the community is that she has forgotten how to have and has become awkward at the thought of a relationship with Mr Norman.

As stated, the Normans have three children, although they will only admit to two. Will Norman – the Normans' eldest son – left home when he was 16 and has not maintained contact with his parents. That was six years ago, and they have lost touch completely. Mrs Norman deals with this by denying Will's existence. Will has become a taboo topic in the Norman household. If Will's name is mentioned, Mrs Norman has one of her bouts of angry depression and Mr Norman has to invest a lot of valuable shed time in trying to talk her round. So Will is not talked about in front of the Normans, although the folk in the village have it on good authority that Will is doing well and is running a reasonably successful media company in North London.

Verity Norman, however, is very much talked about. Verity won scholarships to both Oxford and Cambridge so impressive were her grades. She is in her first year at Oxford studying classics and medieval literature. She is considering following up with a Master's degree in applied mathematics and has plans to go to Brown to study business, Moscow to study ballet and Beijing to study Mandarin. Her parents are, naturally, extraordinarily proud of their daughter.

Here then you have the Normans. Mr Norman is a highly respected businessman/entrepreneur very well regarded in the community. Mrs Norman is beloved by all for her kindness, generosity and willingness to help out in the community. The world has drawn a veil over Will, but Verity shines as a beacon to all daughters. "Who wouldn't be proud of such a family?" say the village folk, "So clever, kind and hard-working, who wouldn't want to be a Norman?" But then they add: "But isn't it a shame about Tim!"

Tim is twenty years old. He lives in his room in a smog of cannabis smoke. He spends most of his day in front of his computer online gaming. *Fortnite*, *Call of Duty*, *Black Ops* and the like. He rarely ventures out of his room and his parents rarely venture in. He is entirely dependent on Mrs Norman who feeds him, does his washing and gives him money. Tim has had a couple of attempts at work when his father arranged internships for him. His father fervently believes that if Tim gets the right job and perhaps a girlfriend all will be well. It is, after all, just a phase: Tim, the Normans tell themselves, always was a bit of a late developer. The jobs tend to last a couple of weeks and then Tim is either asked to leave or decides he 'isn't the sort to work in this environment'. Every so often a strange package drops through the Normans' letterbox post marked Moscow, or Cape Town. Mrs Norman in her innocence of such matters will believe Tim has some new interest, or pen-pal or some such and will enquire nervously about it. "Oh, just a project I'm working on," says Tim and Mrs Norman buys that willingly. Tim has a mate called Nigel who lives in the village and every so often Nigel will ring up. "Hi Nige, yeah, yeah great. Yeah I'll see you in The Fox about Eight. Cheers. Mum, can I borrow twenty quid? I'm going out with Nige."

Mrs Norman gladly gives it to him. "Better take 30 just in case," she says, a little relieved that Tim has some sort of social life. Tim goes out and does not return that evening – nor the evening after or the evening after that. The Normans are frantic with worry. Mrs Norman rings Mr Norman who is on his way back from Brussels. They phone around to no avail. No sign of Tim and the silent spectre of Will haunts the house.

Then at a half past two in the morning, the phone rings.

"Dad, it's me Tim. I'm stuck in Cardiff, and I've no money and I've lost my trousers. Can you come and get me?"

So Mr and Mrs Norman get into the Range Rover and drive to Cardiff to rescue Tim.

THE NORMANS CONSIDERED

Let's look at this. As long as Tim is still there, Mrs Norman doesn't have to face up to the fact that all her children are grown up. The drama of Tim keeps the ghost of Will at bay. Talking about Tim and what to do about him provides a conversation piece, a contact ritual for Mr and Mrs Norman. The only time they talk or do anything together anymore is when they are rescuing Tim. Verity looks even better in the light of Tim who provides a negative role model for her. Below the surface, Tim may know that he is the glue that is keeping his family together.

So what if change is actually introduced into this family system? What happens if Tim gets treatment? What little horrors will be unleashed for the Normans to deal with? How is the intensity and drama of Tim's addiction serving the denial of the family system?

If Tim wakes up one morning and thinks to himself: "This is no life, I've had enough of this!" then goes to his father and asks if he will help pay for treatment, is it not more than likely that Mr Norman will try to dissuade him? "Oh Tim, you don't need that! Those places are filled with the wrong sorts you know. All you need is the proper job and perhaps a nice lady friend. That'll sort you, take my word."

But Tim insists and eventually his father capitulates and Tim goes into treatment.

The family are invited to a family week.

"Oh I don't think we need or want that sort of thing, do we?" says Mr Norman. "After all, it's not you or I that are smoking that weed!" Mrs Norman laughs nervously and agrees.

They don't attend. Tim successfully completes his treatment and chooses to return home where nothing has changed. The systemic undertow – the family dynamics – are such that he will likely be pulled back into his old role as family scapegoat and may well relapse.

How often have I facilitated a family support group that begins in this way? Me: "Good evening everyone, and welcome. Shall we begin by introducing ourselves and saying a bit about why we are here?"

Mr Norman: "Our son, Will, is in treatment for cocaine and ketamine addiction. He's doing very well and we are hoping that he will be home in a couple of weeks. He's been struggling at work and his girlfriend isn't proving very helpful as she says she will leave him unless he controls his drug use. This just seems to stress him more and make things worse. We also recently found out that he's got himself into a lot of debt and that's shocked us a bit. Do you think it'll help him if we pay that off? We are now monitoring his bank accounts so that we can see what he is spending. We're also worried that he might lose his job if he's not careful and so Martha, my wife, has spoken to his boss and explained that Will is having some kind of breakdown but that the psychiatrist says he will recover. He also has ADHD and anxiety which we think is causing his drug use and….."

Me: "Let me stop you there if I may. How are you in all this, Mr Norman? It sounds traumatic for you."

Mr Norman: "Well, he seems to be making progress according to his psychiatrist and the new medication is starting to take effect. He says he is eating properly and doing what is suggested by the nurses and his therapist."

Me: "I asked how *you* were Mr Norman. You must be going through all sorts of hell. May I ask, how old is Tim?"

Mr Norman, with a wry smile that speaks volumes: "He's 38 next birthday."

This kind of conversation happens so very often that I have come to realise that it is symptomatic of family addiction. There is a far more considerable disinclination to *change* a horrific situation than one might suppose. Poor Mr Norman actually doesn't know how he feels except in the context of Tim. His entire sense of self and well-being is dependent upon Tim. If Tim is happy, Mr Norman relaxes somewhat and feels hopeful. If Tim is anxious, Mr Norman feels compelled to act, to *do* something, to fix the situation somehow. If I don't intervene and just let the group run with this, other members will join in and start asking questions about Tim, congratulating him, offering advice and encouragement and so on. If left unchecked, the whole 90-minute group would be taken up with talk of the addicted member and nothing of the families' struggle with anxiety, anger and shame would be mentioned. It is quite alarming to note that, even if I do intervene and encourage the group to talk about themselves, talk keeps moving back to the addict. It is as if the addiction has a kind of gravitational pull, drawing everyone to it. Everybody is implicated in the system which they have built together. They might sometimes say they dislike it, or that they're miserable but they're also attached to it: they *identify* with it.

As mentioned earlier in this book, I will often remind the group that there is also an aftercare support group for the addicts themselves running concurrently and the family group can be sure that they are talking exclusively about their own predicaments, their feelings and their experiences. It is most unlikely that any member of that group will be even thinking about the family and the impact that their addiction has had. So *they* are talking about nothing but themselves and here are we, also talking about them! I even have to tread carefully on occasions because someone will begin to get angry at me and ask what are they supposed to be talking about and they thought they were here to find out how to help the loved one. If I then point out that, in the real world, there is little they can do to help and in truth they are likely to get dragged into a covertly supporting role and end up making matters worse, they might get even angrier.

Then there is the parent whose child is constantly phoning and complaining about the treatment they are receiving in rehab. The parents – Mr and Mrs Norman perhaps – will ask me to comment on the situation. Are the therapists doing the right thing? Their child is not happy and the food is not to their liking and they have had their mobile phone taken away and so on. In such instances, I must repeat that it is time for the parent to step back, stop the constant communication and trust the process: however this attitude or belief is astonishingly stubborn and I will sometimes need to use quite strong interventions to get the point across. Across this country, there are tens of thousands of addicts and alcoholics struggling towards recovery using only AA, NA and the other Twelve Step fellowships. They cannot afford the advantage of professional, inpatient treatment; they may be homeless, without any money and entirely reliant on the considerable goodwill of the fellowships. Yet a significant number of these people get well, in spite of the absence of organic quinoa from their diet or mineral water from Bhutan – or some similar luxury which the five star clinics have added to their programmes.

There is a further complication. I believe that the behaviour I am describing is a relatively recent syndrome and so far only seems to be prevalent in what are called the middle and upper middle classes. These parents appear to hang on to their children well past the age when they have become adults. Notice that Tim in the above example is 38. This is perhaps towards the extreme end of the scale but not so much as you might imagine. It is not uncommon for me to come across parents who are managing the lives, finances, diets and even relationships of their offspring well into their 20s. If I ask those parents how much they had to do with their parents at the same age, they will almost invariably answer: "Oh, almost nothing! I was working and in my own flat by the time I was their age."

This is an important observation. Addicts do not do "difficult"; that is precisely what they avoid by using and drinking and otherwise acting out. This interrupts any genuine emotional development and arrests that development at the age at which the active addiction was triggered. If a parent continues to "help" their afflicted loved one by managing their lives, paying bills and generally standing between them and the true consequences of their addiction, then that parent is in effect obstructing their admittedly painful emotional development. "But he might end up with a criminal record or even in jail." Indeed he might, and that might be the very thing that wakes him or her up. Let it be, the world will do the work and if you as a parent or partner or friend get in the way you are only delaying the inevitable. Perhaps this sounds rather harsh, but remember, when we discuss addiction, we are dealing with a life-threatening condition. This is very serious and the mental health of your whole family is at stake.

So it is now clear that the family members have a tendency to take on powerful and rigid roles as a defence against the painful pathology in the system. For all intents and purposes, the family's response to the addiction constitutes a separate but related addiction in itself. It manifests as an addiction to control and, above all, to *fix*.

We are beginning to mount some powerful arguments in favour of change. I will add another. In my experience, it is not possible for parents or loved ones to treat an addicted family member, the condition is far too serious and one wouldn't dream of treating cancer or heart disease at home. "It" receives all the attention and becomes the powerfully controlling factor in the system, dictating what everyone thinks, feels, believes and how everyone behaves. The intensity and drama of the addicted system is strangely compulsive and addictive in itself and will likely become the norm. Denial is the major symptom of the disease and the family will be in as much – if not more – denial as the addict. The family as a whole needs to enter into their own process of recovery that is separate and distinct from the recovery of the addict. This is important. Lastly, blame is a devastating toxin. Blame clogs up the system like cholesterol in an artery and shuts down all honest communication. No-one is at fault, addiction just happens.

Remember:

You didn't Cause it
You can't Control it
You can't Cure it.

But there is another C word in the equation now and it relates not to 'it' but to yourself. It is Change.

Exercise 4

Make a list of all the things that you really enjoy. Tennis, the theatre, restaurants, having friends round for dinner, anything that brings you any amount of joy. Notice how many of these pleasures have slipped away under the dominion of another's addiction. Be honest with this, remember denial is so very toxic and no-one will judge you. You may be surprised and even shocked at how much you have sacrificed to addiction. It will be appropriate to feel just a little angry at all the addiction has taken from you.

Every week, choose one of the activities on this list and promise yourself to re-instate it. It might be you and your partner go out for dinner, or you go swimming with a friend, it doesn't matter and it does not need to be a big thing. See this as you beginning to re-claim your life from the tyranny of addiction.

CHAPTER 5

WHAT ON EARTH CAN I DO NOW?

A fakir claimed that he could teach any illiterate person to read through an "instant technique."

"OK," Nasrudin said. "Teach me."

The fakir then touched Nasrudin's head and said, "Now go read something."

Nasrudin left, and returned to the village square an hour later with an angry look on his face.

"What happened?" asked the villagers. "Can you read now?"

"Indeed I can," replied Nasrudin, "but that's not why I came back. Now where is that scoundrel fakir?"

"Mulla," the people said, "he taught you to read in no more than a minute. So what makes you think he's a scoundrel?"

"Well," Nasrudin explained, "I was just reading a book that asserted: 'All fakirs are frauds.'

Case History 5

Muriel came to see me about her husband Dexter. He was, she said, suffering with stress, anxiety and depression. Whenever I hear those three words, a voice in my head goes "Uh-Oh!" and I wait for what invariably comes next.

"I think Dexter has underlying trauma issues from his childhood and is trying to manage them."

"I see." I reply: "What are you seeing, Muriel, that leads you to this point?"

"Well, he is drinking a lot more and I think he might be using something else."

"What makes you think that Muriel?"

"He doesn't seem himself, he's angry all the time and often horrid to me." Tears start in her eyes at this.

"Oh I'm sorry. How is he horrid?"

"He's angry and blames me for all sorts. I think he watches porn and if I confront him he says it's because I'm not sexy enough or attractive and he doesn't fancy me anymore. I do try to make myself prettier and sexier, but it's not easy when you have two young kids."

My heart goes out to Muriel.

"What does Dexter do for a career?"

"He's a barrister. He is very clever and good at arguing his case."

"What do you mean Muriel?"

"He is very good at pointing out where I am wrong and making me feel stupid."

I am starting to roundly dislike Dexter, and have to remind myself that we are likely dealing with addiction and that this is not a condition of identity.

"Can you give me an example of how he does this?"

"Well, it's embarrassing to talk about."

"Just do your best Muriel."

"Last weekend, he didn't come home on the Saturday night. He said he was meeting some friends and might be a bit late home. That's nothing new, he's often late home. Anyway, I asked him if he was alright and where had he been. He just turned on me." Muriel began to cry.

"What the f*** is that to do with you, you stupid cow. Leave me alone, just f*** off and leave me alone.' The kids heard him yelling and started crying. I didn't know what to do, I was so upset."

Upset is a word I hear so often.

"What does upset mean Muriel?"

"I hated him just then. I was tired and frightened and trying to look after the children. I was furious."

"What stopped you telling him?"

"I don't know." She seemed to regain her composure. "How would that help? It's wrong to hate someone, isn't it? And getting so angry is wrong too."

"Muriel, do you know what cocaine is?"

"Yes....."

"And do you know where your husband was on that Saturday night?"

"Yes....."

"That wasn't the first time either?"

"No. I feel so ashamed. He takes cocaine. He drinks and he sees prostitutes! He tells me it's because of me and perhaps he's right. I'm exhausted and worn away!"

"Muriel, Dexter's anxiety and depression are symptoms of his addiction and his 'underlying issues' simply don't matter at this point. He is drinking, using cocaine and acting out sexually. It is not your fault, not in any way, shape or form. He is sick and in the way that you might be thinking, you cannot help him. Trying to change yourself into what you think he wants will really hurt you and have no effect on him. It's time for you to begin to look after yourself."

"How can I do that? I have the children and he says it's his family and his house. I sometimes wish I could take the kids somewhere away from him."

"Is there anywhere you could go?"

After a few weeks of working with Muriel, she was able to take her and the children to stay with friends in Ireland. She had told Dexter that she could no longer live like this and he needed help – help that she could not give. She told him she loved him and that she still wanted their marriage to work but that she needed to look after herself and the children by removing herself from what had become a very toxic situation. She asked him to get real help with his addiction.

Two years on, Dexter has been clean and sober for nine months and Muriel recognising that early recovery is not yet normal life, maintains her boundaries and still lives separately, but with a view to re-negotiating family life in the near future.

WORKING UPON YOURSELF

In the last chapter we resolved upon some kind of change. In this chapter we need to go deeper into what that might mean. It would be reasonable to suggest that with this book, that my task is to get you to work on yourselves rather than think of how to make others do what you want them to do.

Let's be honest. You have tried and tried to fix this, and the evidence of success is so limited as to be negligible. You may have tried hiding bottles, visiting the local corner shop and begging them not to serve the loved one alcohol. You may have purloined mobile phones and pleaded with dealers. You may have tried testing them, mounted a 24 hour rotating watch on them, locked them in the cellar, offered rewards, money, flats, ponies and goodness knows what. You might have found a way of remotely logging into their phone or tablet so that now you are able to watch helplessly as the true terror of the situation unfolds before you in real time, and believe me, however bad you *think* it is, the reality will certainly be worse and now you have the ghastly truth, and there is nothing you can do with it!

Whatever you may have tried, it probably hasn't worked, and so you turn up the volume and do more of what you have already done only louder and harder. You might bring in GPs, psychiatrists, therapists, shamans; suggest medication, religion, meditation, girl or boyfriends, internships, or some sort of self-discovery trip around the world on a tall ship. It doesn't work and the situation worsens because the way is shut. Confronting the impossible is the only way through – and we have resolved on that.

So now that we have decided to change the situation, what can actually be done? The first step of the Twelve Steps of Alcoholics Anonymous is this: "We Admitted We Were Powerless Over Alcohol, That Our Lives Had Become Unmanageable." This step applies to family members as much as it does to the alcoholic or the addict. We have seen previous chapters how we have become reliant on a set of thoughts, feelings and behaviours that we fondly believe are effective and will keep us safe. These ways of reacting quickly become automatic and indeed mechanical thereby becoming covertly harmful and counter-productive. Conditioning gives rise to "supermarket" thinking and feeling that comes from the herd and not from you as an individual human entity in planetary life. Supermarket thinking is a lazy form of associative flow that is often taken for logic, common sense and reason. It is, however, a mish mash of hearsay, opinion and prejudice which has nothing to do with real thinking.

Real thinking requires effort and suffering. An excellent starting point for what might be called real thinking is simply "I don't know!" so let's start there. Change begins in something like this acknowledgement. We have to accept our powerlessness.

UPON RUMPELSTILTSKIN

Let's bring in the Brothers Grimm again. In the famous story of Rumpelstiltskin, we have a beautiful picture of powerlessness.

Let's remind ourselves of this story but consider it through the eyes of addiction. An avaricious and self-seeking miller offers his daughter in marriage to a prince. He awakens the prince's interest in his daughter by boasting to him that she can spin straw into gold. This, sadly, she cannot really do, but the prince is intrigued and carries the daughter off to his palace and locks her in a room full of straw and a spinning wheel with the admonition that she should spin the straw into gold by morning. If she does so, he will marry her but if not he will chop off her head! Anyway, the poor girl tries her best – but of course there is no possibility of her spinning the ghastly stuff into gold. So she does nothing except weep and weep, because there is nothing else she can do. And doing nothing does the trick: she gives up and in herself confronts the impossible.

No sooner does she do this than out of nowhere real help arrives in the shape of an ugly little man. The little man visits three times and on the first two occasions the daughter rewards him with a necklace or a ring. But on the third visit, he asks for her firstborn as a reward. She, mindful of her head, agrees. The ugly little man is not so bad at all, when the daughter's first born arrives he shows up and she pleads with him not to take it and he, very reasonably in my view and given the circumstances, gives her three days and three chances to guess his name. I'm sure you know what happens next. The first two chances are quite wrong, but on the third day, a servant who is searching for a clue comes across the little chap in "The forest behind the mountains where the fox and the hare say goodnight". There he learns the name Rumpelstiltskin and the rest, so to speak is history and the enviable condition known as "Happy Ever After" is invoked for all.

Now the miller's daughter may well have thought herself very lucky, but luck had nothing to do with it: by making a positive move in the direction of admitting her own helplessness the miller's daughter changed the dynamic until Rumpelstiltskin had to tell her his name. An element of Necessity was introduced. This story occurs everywhere and always the name is known at last. In England it is Tom Tit Tot, Whuppety Stoorey in Scotland, Vargaluska in Russia and in Africa he is a hippopotamus called Mr. Johnson.

So this wonderful tale is full of clues which might help us understand how to approach the conundrum of being caught up in a family system where addiction is King. I wish everyone would read these stories and reclaim them from the unappreciative clutches of our children! The miller's daughter has no choice but to accept her powerlessness, and when she does so another level is activated: the all-important name was discovered in the forest behind the mountains – a place on a different level also known as East of the Sun, West of the Moon. This other level, that can only be activated when the impossible is confronted, is to be found in every culture across the globe and across the centuries. Messengers or agents from this level may take the shape of a frog, a fox, a woodsman, an old woman, or something else – but they always come.

There is no solid and practical solution to the so-called problem. This is what makes acknowledgment of powerlessness over addiction such an important step. It constitutes a move away from the bafflement that has been suffocating you, and taking you away from all the things you have loved in life. The obverse course, making the process about what you *need*, rather than about what you need to *accept* simply doesn't work. This is for the simple reason that your own anxiety, shame, and sense of failure are probably driving the need to fix. Over time, everyone will get into the toxic way of needing to be right, and this collective need will override any genuinely helpful conversations about real solutions: no-one in the system will have ears to listen. The family will split into warring factions, each according to their particular opinions and prejudices whilst the addiction holds sway and controls everything.

Humility is a much-maligned quality, yet here it is at the centre of this new phase in your response to addiction.

WHAT IS POWERLESSNESS?

Of course, it's all very well for me to say that you need to let go, and that all will be well. We might need to know more about powerlessness and more about humility, and what these really entail in order to do that. When we do this we must remind ourselves the importance of what we're attempting to do here: it's only with humility that comes access to the forest behind the mountain.

Powerlessness is difficult to do in the right way, because it is not some sort of isolated quick fix. It is not a feeling – rather it is a state to which certain powerfully negative emotions attach. Shame, anxiety, guilt, anger and loneliness all cluster around powerlessness like so many wasps. As a general rule, these feelings then drive certain compulsive and maladaptive behaviours. However, since we now know that powerlessness is so necessary, we realise now that we need to push on through in order to reach the next stage in our lives. Coming into powerlessness involves letting go of outcomes and if we do that we have to face certain frightening possibilities, and I'm afraid there always is a realistic possibility that terrible things will happen to the addict no matter what anyone does, including you, once the addiction has taken hold. If we do not take this difficult step, we will always be trying to control the situation so that we do not have to face reality and the terrors that come with it. We need support in this and the wisdom of others who have gone before.

There is a sort of paradox housed in humility. In one sense it might sound in some way passive, in that it has to do with not doing things which you are accustomed to doing: essentially seeking to fix and control the situation. But it gives rise also to a new or remembered faculty which is anything but passive: we begin over time to change ourselves – by humility, by powerlessness, we make room for that change.

But, of course, as soon as we do this, we are exposed to all that we can't control – and though we have now accepted that seeking to control it is no longer in our interests, we are now exposed to all the things that can happen by our stepping into this vital new set of attitudes which I am describing. I call this the knotty problem of *unmanageability*. External unmanageability might be defined as all the things that might or will happen which are absolutely beyond your control. This might manifest as debt, family feuds, violence, divorce, loss of jobs, breakdown of relationships and so forth. The list is long, and it's not a pleasant read. It may be that a well-resourced family system does not feel the pinch of unmanageability at first, but over time I can guarantee that everybody does. Nobody can be cocooned from the painful aspects of life by wealth, power, status or indeed by anything else.

In short, bad things will happen once addiction is in the picture. Perhaps social services or the police will become involved in a safeguarding issue. Perhaps an enraged drug dealer will smash down the front door of your beautiful West Dulwich house at 3am. Or it could be that you will find yourself in an expensive divorce lawyer's office, on the clock for £600 an hour.

But if you consider a moment, I think you will agree that internal unmanageability, which is what you've been living with, and what you've resolved to move away from, is worse than anything external unmanageability can throw at you. That's because internal unmanageability involves, as we have seen in the early chapters of this book, the loss of control of one's emotions whereby anxiety, shame, anger and guilt come to rule your life. In that scenario, all your actions are driven by powerful negative forces. As we have seen, this leads inexorably to a covert, parallel addiction. The addicted family member uses substances or behaviour to manage overwhelmingly difficult feelings and the family member uses control to change or fix the addict.

If we don't want this – and we've decided in the last chapter that we don't – then we have to choose external unmanageability.

THE VITAL IMPORTANCE OF MAKING THE ATTEMPT

I am often told that this move away from control towards an acceptance of powerlessness is too hard. Actually, it is only that we think it is – and in any case, it isn't possible to say we can't do something when we haven't even tried to do it. When we project ourselves into the impossibility of beginning all we are really doing is making up stories. "Can't" in most cases might really be translated as "won't" – or "I don't want to". You are not given that which you cannot bear. It is so easy to think, "This is too much for me". In my experience, it never is, if you take things as they come. This is an important part of beginning change – not to try to predict outcomes, and peer round corners. You are not clairvoyant and will only be using your imagination to create a set of scenarios which will not happen. It is far better to admit powerlessness, and not think about what that admission might do for your future self. Do it instead for you today. But perhaps it will help you to know as you make this short term step that miracles happen to be the currency of the Forest Behind the Mountains, The Nine Time Lands of the Wonder Tales. But don't spend time now imagining what kind of miracles you might benefit from in the future.

Instead let's concentrate on practical steps. First and foremost, we need to take the focus of the system away from the addiction. If you are a parent with an addicted child who has siblings, the chances are the siblings will be feeling neglected as they watch all the financial and emotional resources disappearing down a black hole. In addition to that, your world has likely become increasingly narrow and limited as you allow the addiction to dictate what you think, feel and do. As an example: "Can we go on holiday this year?" "Well I really don't think we should. If we do go we can't leave them here and if we take them with us, they will just take over the holiday." In that example again, what is really meant by 'can't' is 'won't'. In saying, I won't go on holiday you are taking ownership, it is an internal decision. If you say I can't then you are placing the power of choice outside of yourself and heading down the slippery slope to victimhood. In my career, I have seen this attitude continue even if the identified addict goes into treatment. Your addicted loved one may be there, surrounded by therapists, nurses, and other group members – and as secure and safe as they will ever be. Yet you still feel the need to be at home, just in case.

But just in case of what? For the family, this has to change: you cannot continue to allow the devastating pathology of addiction to rule your life and the lives of those near to you. So this is the first change to make: to think of yourself first, and not of the identified addict.

Now that you are definitely resolved to make this attempt you need to begin to set boundaries.

A BRIEF GUIDE IN HOW TO BOUNDARY SET

Boundaries tend to be widely misunderstood. They are not put in place to change another's behaviour: they are put in place to protect you and the family from the aberrant and harmful behaviour of others. They are also there to protect others from your own pathological behaviours.

The need to do this in no way reflects badly on you. I believe that almost everyone on the planet is really rather crazy. This is our lot – and in fact it is the raw material – the soil – out of which we can begin to grow. Being crazy isn't the problem – pretending not to be is. And if we were fairly mad to begin with, then addiction just went and made us a whole lot crazier, meaning that some sort of fundamental shift is necessary and appropriate. This is what boundary work is.

In fact, I would go as far as to say that boundaries, both internal and external – sticking resolutely to them through thick and thin – is the fundamental work at the beginning of your recovery. Boundaries give you shape, they prevent you collapsing into intensity and unmanageable feelings: they stop you spilling out your rage, terror and shame onto others and back into the system. Boundaries also have this inestimable benefit: they require you to take ownership and therefore responsibility for your negative emotions and feelings, and in addition to that also allow you to choose your responses. They permit you to revisit the crucial question of who you are. Realistic boundaries put you in charge of your world; you can choose to respond as a human rather than react as a machine. This is very important. There are plenty of very good books and articles about how to set and hold boundaries and so I won't go into greater detail here, just suffice it to say that the hidden benefits to you of this difficult yet rewarding process are many and rich.

DETACHING FROM NEGATIVE STATES

What does taking responsibility look like? It can be a difficult and sometimes daunting process; however, it is deeply rewarding and the changes for the better that can come about as a consequence could be described as extraordinary.

After some sort of acknowledgment of powerlessness in the situation, and some preliminary boundary-setting, taking responsibility progresses through a willingness to have a more open mind. This is a dangerous moment, and fraught with shame, anger and resentment, all of which tend to make a return to inertia possible. And so we need to go to work on these. If I am angry, for example, that anger is in me, and though I might not think so, I do have a choice about what to do with it. I can detach from the anger rather than have anger run the show. This is really no more than the old "count to ten" admonition. If I refuse or am unable to manage this choice in a positive fashion, I may lose my "shape" and collapse into that emotion. We need to realise that all dangerously negative states are exclusively internal; they are in us and not in the outside world. Road rage is a good example of our strange propensity for futile emotion. From a calm distance, we may see how fruitless and energy-consuming this way of being in the world is, but once we become attached it is oddly addictive. These negative forces are exhausting; they consume energy, leaving us drained and useless.

On the other hand, there's some good news here too. These seemingly negative feelings are the shadow side of very positive feelings. For example shame is the dark side of healthy remorse and thus dignity. Anger is also a powerful agent for positive change and creativity if used in the right way.

So, who gets to choose? This is an important question, simply answered. *You* get to choose:

You not the anger
You not the fear
You not the shame.

As you detach from these dangerous states, you cease to become mechanical. Instead of reacting in the same, predictable way and probably with the same consequences, you begin to discover your ability to respond, to be creative or even, like the Miller's Daughter, to do nothing if nothing can be done in the situation. This might not be the change you were expecting in the last chapter, but it is a change, and one with huge potential. This is the struggle towards a life we want, and just by your doing it, the family dynamics will begin to change. Instead of intense drama, calm and order dawns on the horizon, hope and optimism begin to arise in the place of despair and desperation.

THE POWER OF 'SO WHAT'

George Gurdjieff (c. 1867-1949) was an Armenian philosopher who thought very deeply about all of the things I am discussing. He referred to the importance of addressing the issue of "internal considering" – or fear of what other people think – when it comes to enacting improvements in ourselves. I believe this is one of the great afflictions of mankind and leads nowhere but to hopeless self-centred anxiety.

Dare to look into yourself for a moment and see how much internal considering may be affecting your life and the lives of those around you. It is worth noting too that the stigma and opprobrium attached to addiction do nothing but nourish this ghastly and pervasive affliction, and yet we can here, as in our last section, choose not to act on the fear. It will entail realising the truth of the following statement:

It really doesn't matter what anyone else thinks about your situation.

A remarkably effective antidote to the traps and pitfalls of internal considering is judicious use of the power of: So What? If you are concerned about what you think the neighbours might be thinking or what the other mothers on the school run are saying try using the power of So What?

The more you can realise that the opinions of others don't matter, the more you can free up energy to focus on what does: your own happiness.

It is important to stress however that patience, persistence and kindness to self are vital prerequisites in this process. As tempting as it will be, you must not attempt to bully yourself into recovery. Not only will that not work but you will hurt yourself and make matters worse. By choosing to change the situation by working on yourself, you haven't found an instant fix. In fact, you are entering a lengthy, sometimes painful, but ultimately rich and rewarding process, whose time scales sometimes act slowly.

A BRIEF DISCOURSE ON LEAVING PRISON

What three things do you need to escape from prison?

The first thing is to recognise and *feel* that you are in prison. This can be most unpleasant: the realisation of your true situation might come as quite a shock. But what else have we been describing throughout this book than imprisonment? Now we are awake we can begin to plan our escape.

What is this prison? It is nothing other than you – or rather your small frightened survival self – with all its wounds, beliefs, habits and attachments. In the case of the addicted family system, this little self is likely to have become compulsive, dogmatic and very brittle. What do you think will happen if you begin to let go of some of the things in the "big bag of stuff" which we mentioned in the previous chapters? The prison in which we find ourselves is constructed from this "stuff" and the jailers are our fear, shame, anger, hatred and guilt. This makes escape tricky because anyone who has already escaped and tries to help you will have to deal with these jailers. These jailers have a dark power; they can masquerade as truth and reality.

THE IMPORTANCE OF THIRD FORCE

Any genuine attempt to escape from prison will activate these jailers. I believe it was Sir Isaac Newton who wisely observed that every action has an equal and opposite reaction. What he did not mention is that for anything to be completed a third, balancing force is required.

For instance, how often have you begun a project with great energy and enthusiasm only to have that project torpedoed by circumstance or by criticism or by faint praise? It seems to be a universal principle that as soon as you begin something – and this is especially the case with a project as gigantic as trying to fix yourself in the addiction context – you automatically invoke its opposite and will at some point need to apply the third force to keep the momentum going.

Let me illustrate. Imagine a soul in the grip of alcoholism. From somewhere, perhaps from family or perhaps from friends, this soul receives an impulse which generates a sufficiently significant metanoia so that the sufferer makes a relatively deep decision to seek help. This they do and find themselves in rehab and, subsequently, in recovery. They have enthusiasm and energy for their new-found sobriety and commit themselves to a programme of 12-step meetings. This is working well, everyone is hopeful, life is stabilising and returning to a happyish status quo.

But then something happens. We might follow Mr Gurdjieff and call this the denying force.

Let's say recovering addict's wife goes away on a business trip or a pre-arranged holiday with friends. Competing voices will seek to drag that addict back to prison: "She's not here, no-one will know. You can have one drink: it'll be fine." "How can she abandon you at this point, doesn't she realise how vulnerable you are?" And so on and so forth. If the suffering addict is not alert to these devils, he or she will likely relapse. But by introducing a third and balancing force, there is a very good chance that the sufferer will be able to maintain sanity and sobriety and resist the wiles of the internal jailers. Now what might in this instance constitute third force? It could be attendance at an AA meeting, phoning a friend who understands, or it could be reading some sort of helpful literature.

In the above paragraph, I have intentionally framed this explanation from the perspective of the addict – but exactly the same process applies to the family member. We must enter into this process of boundary setting, being kind to ourselves, and refusing to mind what others' think, in full awareness that the internal jailers of the family member may be even more alert and readily mobilised than those of the addict.

Let's try another example. Imagine a mother, whose beloved son is in residential treatment. She has attended Al Anon, family support groups and is now therapeutically detached and has her boundaries well in place. She is determined not to collapse into controlling and "fixing". There is an interesting programme on BBC Radio Four about the myth of residential treatment and how it may not be as effective as is generally believed. She becomes edgy and anxious. What if she has made a mistake? Is her loved one in safe hands? The telephone rings and her heart skips a beat as she sees it is from her child (who actually happens to be 25).

"Gregory, is everything alright?"

"Not really mum, I hate it here, it's a boot camp. They even make us wash up, and I have to share a room with someone from Moldova!"

Before the scholarly folks at Radio Four had stuck their academic oar in, she would have had the strength and the wit to respond appropriately: "Well, I'm sorry to hear you are finding treatment troublesome; however, it's best you take your difficulties to your therapist and your group."

But now, she panics: "Oh my goodness Gregory. Just sit still and wait there, your father and I will fly out to Cape Town tonight and get you out of there!"

This sort of thing does happen and with inevitably ghastly consequences. By the time Mum and Dad get to Cape Town, Gregory is in a ketamine-induced haze, calm in the knowledge that rescue is on its way. The mother's internal jailers have triumphed; her fear, shame and guilt have dragged her back to prison and her original false reliance on maladaptive patterns.

Let's go back to Rumpelstiltskin. The Miller's daughter, through no fault of her own, is faced with the impossible. She does nothing, for there is nothing she can do, and so she activates something "other" and receives the help she so badly needs. A degree of reflection will show you that the goblin man was playing his part in the bigger drama. After all, he did allow the Miller's daughter to change the contract, so to speak, and load it in her favour and in the end, it was he himself who gave his name away. Our third force needs to contain an awareness of all this – that no matter what, we shall push on through. We have chosen our course, and we know a little about it – and we certainly know that we mustn't renege, because if we do we'll be back to square one.

Exercise 5

On a blank piece of paper draw a line to make two columns. Label the left hand column " I WILL" and the right hand column "I WILL NOT".

This is where I ask you to be as honest as you can with yourself. You may be thinking this is a list of things you need to do and things you need to stop doing, but it isn't that; this is an inventory of actions and behaviours that are *already in place*.

For example, you may be taking your addict son coffee and chocolate croissant to wake them in the morning. If this is the case, that goes in the I WILL column. If you are reluctant to call the police when your spouse has taken the car and you know full well they are drink-driving, this will go in the I WILL NOT. Be as thorough as you may with this inventory. Then set it aside for three days. Return to your list and see if there are other things to be added. After another three days, take your list and resolve to move one item from the I WILL list to the I WILL NOT column. As you do so, say to yourself: "I wish very much to make and hold this change".

Let's say you have resolved to stop with the coffee and croissant, now you must hold this boundary even in the face of complaints, abuse and whatever else.

Every three days, move another item from I WILL to I WILL NOT.
Some example might be:
Give them money.
Answer every text or phone call as soon as possible.
Phone them three times every day.
Track their phone.
Let them live rent free in your home.

There are, of course , many more possibilities. The goal of this exercise is to look closely at the structure of your life as it relates to the presence of addiction.

SIX IMPOSSIBLE THINGS
BEFORE BREAKFAST

Nasrudin was very ill and his wife, thinking he was dying, called for the Imam to administer the last rites. "Nasrudin," said the Imam. "Do you here and now renounce Satan and all his works. Do you humbly and earnestly beg Allah for mercy?"

"Well," said Nasrudin thoughtfully, "I would except that at this moment, I don't want to make any enemies!"

*

"We need, in love, to practice only this: letting each other go. For holding on comes easily; we do not need to learn it."

Rainer Maria Rilke

*

"I see that I never allow an experience to take place in myself. I always resist the full experience. This is because I want to lead it. I do not trust the experience, I trust only me. Because of this, it does not transform me. When I begin to perceive a subtle Presence in myself, I feel it as something alive that

calls for its action to be felt. But I cannot feel its action deeply because I am separated from it by a wall of tensions, that is, of my mental reactions."

Jeanne de Salzmann, 'The Reality of Being'

Case History 6

More or less forty years ago I stepped out of the howling wilderness of drugs and drink. I had been a moderately successful guitar player and had made my living from rock and roll, of a sort. That had all been swept away. I found myself in early recovery with nothing and with none of those quali-fications that the normal world sees as important. I had been expelled from grammar school at 15. Nevertheless, I had clawed my way back to some rudimentary form of what one might call normal life. I had employment. I was working as a care assistant in the psycho-geriatric ward of a local psychiatric hospital; I was what was known as a "Poo Droid". The majority of the job involved dealing with human excrement in one form or another.

As you can imagine, this was not an ideal situation. I had at least a council flat and somewhere to sleep and just about enough money to avoid starvation. So I started to wonder what to do with my life. I was clean and sober but that was it. I began to play with the idea of becoming some kind of addiction therapist: after all, I knew quite a lot about all that. The idea grew and I began to look for ways and means to make the notion manifest. Bear in mind this was in the days before the Internet and research had to be conducted in libraries and similar institutions. I found courses that trained addiction counsellors and one in particular caught my eye. It was a year-long live-in training and internship at a centre called Clouds House in Wiltshire. Clouds at that time had a very high reputation. I applied and, to my aston-ishment, after a gruelling two-day interview I was accepted onto the course and offered a place for the next year, starting in March. This was in May of the year before. There was one huge and seemingly insurmountable obstacle. The course was very expensive.

During my childhood, into my teens and into my twenties, I had had a love for the work of C.S Lewis. I found his writings both comforting and inspiring, starting with Narnia and on to his space trilogy and beyond. I had somehow come to rely on him as a source of guidance and comfort. About this time, a film called *Shadowlands*, about the life of C.S Lewis had been released and was now available on video from Blockbuster. It starred Sir Anthony Hopkins as Lewis. I loved it and watched it over and over again.

Somehow I had to raise the large amount of money to pay for the training. I could not borrow, was not eligible for any grants, and so I went to the library and went through a publication called Spotlight that had details of how to get in touch with famous people. Then I sat down and hand wrote literally hundreds of letters. Over the next weeks and months I had lots of replies, mostly encouraging and kind, but still no offers of help.

By Christmas, the replies had dried up. I was feeling hopeless and desperate, as though a huge iron door were closing on any future I might have been foolish enough to imagine. I could not go on as I was, and so I thought I would just show up at Clouds in March and see what happened. It might be that by the time they had got round to realising I hadn't paid, something might have happened.

At the beginning of March, literally two weeks before the start of the course something did happen. I was committed to a leap into nothing. I had packed up my stuff and given notice on my council flat. It was all or nothing. Like the miller's daughter in Rumpelstiltskin I stood at the closed door of the impossible. And it opened. The next morning a letter came. I had a strange prescience and opened it with shaking hands.

"Dear Francis," it read: "Congratulations on being accepted on the course. Sir Anthony would like to pay your fees."

THE GOLDEN BIRD

Step two of The Twelve Steps of Alcoholics Anonymous states that: "We Came To Believe That A Power Greater Than Ourselves Could Restore Us To Sanity."

Interestingly, the Grimm's tale called 'The Golden Bird' encircles this very notion. You might know the story but it never hurts to recall it. A King had a tree that gave golden apples – but, as they ripened, they began to disappear one by one. The King ordered the gardener to keep watch, but the gardener fell asleep at midnight, and another apple went missing. The gardener orders his first son to guard the tree, but the same thing happens. So the gardener's second son has a go with the same outcome.

The gardener's third son, however, stays awake and watches as a golden bird comes and steals an apple. The boy fires an arrow at the bird, but only manages to shoot off a single golden feather which the boy brings to the King. Of course, the king demands the whole bird and sends his eldest son out to find the bird. At the edge of a forest, the eldest son encounters a fox and the son grabs his rifle and takes aim – but the fox starts speaking. "Don't shoot and I'll give you some good advice. I know where you are going. Soon you will come to a village with two inns. One will be brightly lit with a great deal of merrymaking going on inside. Don't go there! Instead go to the other inn, be it ne'er so dismal!"

The king's son laughs, pulls the trigger and, fortunately, misses the fox. By evening, he came to the village with the two inns, and being who he is, he enters the first inn. That's him out of the tale for a while. The second son then sets out, meets the fox and the same thing happens. The third and youngest son, sets off and encounters the fox and being a good-natured chap, he listens to the fox who tells him to climb upon his tail. This he does and they set off "over sticks and stones so swiftly that the wind whistled through the prince's hair."

They came to the village and the prince, following the fox's advice, chooses the dismal inn. The next morning, the prince found the fox waiting for him. The prince, after following the first piece of advice, subsequently does exactly the opposite to what the fox tells him in every case. However, the patient fox rescues him time after time until he attains the condition of Happy Ever After. At that moment, the fox asks him to cut off his paws and his head. After considerable agonising, the prince does the deed and behold! The fox is transformed into a handsome prince.

PURPOSE AND ORIGIN

A question I often like to ask in the family groups that I run goes like this: Your little girl or boy, say age three or four, asks you "Where do babies come from Mummy and Daddy?" How do you answer? Invariably, there are two sets of answers; one set centres around a biological notion of eggs and sperm and the other around some quite vague conundrum of what happens when two people are in love, again often collapsing into a biological paradigm. I am far from sure that this is what the little one is asking.

Perhaps they are wondering who they are, and what they are doing here. These are very valid and indeed important questions that demand better than a stock supermarket response.

The great Sufi master, Jalaludin Rumi, when asked where he had come from, famously responded: "I came out of nothing, trailing stars." At its heart, life is a great mystery and it is not the least of the cruelties of addiction that it tends to deprive us of this beautiful sense of partaking in vast cosmic processes. The growth of the child in the womb is a miraculous undertaking. Is there any reason to believe that this wondrous process should suddenly cease at birth? As I write this it is St Brigid's day, the day of quickening when nature begins to awake; when the bright energies of spring pour out love potions upon the stirring earth. Where I live in Dorset, the snowdrops are showing. Soon there will be primroses, crocuses and daffodils. After that will come the blackthorn and the May blossom. There is no board or committee overseeing this awakening and no government agency intervening to mess it up. You and I are a part of this living reality: all around us there is growth, and quiet healing. If you cut your finger with a knife, it will heal. If you eat a delicious meal, it is digested for you. You decide to run a half-marathon. The movement, breathing and everything else is done for you by something which you most certainly take for granted and do not understand. Everything about the mundane turns out to be startling and strange, and when we begin to heal from the pain of addiction one of the joys is that we can become aware of all this again.

How do we align with all this? As you move out of the crisis of addiction, it will help to pay attention to things. The hawthorn trees along the River Stour nearby to where I live will produce the best and most abundant blossoms that they can without a morsel of low self-esteem or faux modesty. Under the influence of the great drive of life, they will simply go for it: we need to learn to do the same, to realise the governing power of things greater than ourselves. This means the humility of exploring, and not trying to micromanage our own process. We are not in the driver's seat, nor were we meant to be.

As we have seen, the difficulty for families in which the djinn of addiction has been released from its Solomon's bottle is that there is an overwhelming temptation to lead, and to seek to control the process of recovery. We have seen over the course of this book that that can't be done. So what is the flipside of this realisation? It is that we all have our own contract with the cosmos with which none may interfere. This knowledge releases us into humility; it brings us more into line with the true pattern of things. There, we have believed six impossible things before breakfast.

THE ELEPHANT IN THE ROOM

"Yes, but what do I do?" I hear you cry.

Purely out of curiosity, I turned to Google for a definition of "spirituality". There are some quite extraordinary ideas out there, but I can compile a list of words/practices that seem to be common to most definitions: awakening, meditation, mindfulness, Christianity, Buddhism and so on. It would be foolish of me to naysay any of these practices. But I think the idea of spiritual awakening has come to mean something rather too cosy, and we must be prepared for the notion that as we awaken from the sleep of addiction, and our own complicity in it, that there won't be choirs of angels singing.

It doesn't quite work that way. It's in fact a ghastly experience, as one begins to realise at a deep level what one is actually like and the reality of one's situation. Inscribed in the Temple of Apollo in Delphi in ancient Greece was the Socratic injunction to "Know Thyself". Perhaps the quest to know oneself, truly know oneself, is the way of practical spirituality.

In active addiction, the afflicted individual relates to their substance or behaviour with a religious devotion – and it is this which means they have lost all contact with their true selves: their drink, drug or action becomes their higher power and they truly believe that it will "restore them to sanity", or at least give them the temporary and subjective experience of normality. In time, as we have seen, the addiction becomes the higher power of the family system and so it now stands to reason that you will need another higher power really to fight that addiction. This has to be a new and functional higher power that does not rule the family with fear and shame. This needn't have anything to do with religion. For the actual addict, a new and higher power needs only to be something that has more importance and significance than their drink or drug use and can exert some leverage in times of crisis. It is the same for the family members. What is required is some principle, action or even material that is allowed to matter more than fixing the addiction.

Some examples can be very prosaic indeed. It might be a holiday. Let's return to our example in the previous chapter, whereby a planned holiday has been put on indefinite hold because of an addicted loved one. If that holiday becomes a higher power and a point of reference for the system it can have very positive effects. If the addicted one is living with you, it may provide the energy and will to take the necessary step of asking them to leave, if they are, for example, exhibiting dangerous tendencies of dependency and are easily old enough to leave home. The resulting holiday will involve the family in planning, anticipating and perhaps even getting excited about the holiday. Or it might be something else. Instead of spending your money on bailing the addict out, paying his or her rent, feeding them and so on, think about buying the car you have always wanted, or paying for that improving course you have been hankering after for so long.

THE FRONT LINES OF THE ANTI-FEELINGS PARADIGM

We in what is called the West live neck up in what might be termed an anti-feelings paradigm. There is a belief prevalent across medicine, therapy and in life-coaching that difficult, unpleasant and painful feelings are a problem that needs fixing. This fix might take any number of forms: it may involve medication, or some kind of therapeutic programme, or some misunderstood spiritual path or practice. In my own view and experience this is a grave error. One cannot use spiritual ideas to avoid painful and difficult feelings. If we do, then we risk engendering a kind of zombie apocalypse when all the feelings we thought we had buried arise from their graves and infect every aspect of our lives: when we bury feelings, we bury them alive.

Of course, the idea that if we change our thinking, our feelings will change accordingly has value, but this will only apply in a few limited circumstances. Try thinking your way out of deep, shame-based low self-worth – or grief or deep depression for that matter. In actual fact, it is not so much the feelings that are the problem, it is rather the relationship we have with them that leads to so many difficulties. Spiritual ideas should, if they are genuine, bring you face-to-face with a sort of unwarranted darkness which we have allowed to rise up and dominate us. Any spiritual or moral system worth its salt must provide us with a new lens with which to view what is happening in the shadows of ourselves.

All this takes courage and a certain strength. But these qualities can be acquired and will prove to be keystones of a new and more open relationship with oneself.

HOW DO WE EFFECT TRANSFORMATION?

It follows from all of the above that every time you act upon a powerful negative feeling you abdicate your own selfhood. You lose all shape and collapse, like a punctured water balloon, into a pool of whatever emotion it may be that is assailing you. Under such circumstances, you as a human being are no longer in control: you have become a weapon wielded by the hands of fear – or hate or anger or shame.

But the opposite of the dark situation I am describing is light. Well then, where is light to be found in the predicament of the family in which addiction has come to hold sway?

Actually, there is a way and it can be termed self-observation. What needs to happen is that you need to separate some part of yourself from the rest: this part may then strive to become impartial and disengaged from the overall gallop of dark feelings and allow there to be a degree of choice.

This can be done more readily if the light of joy, calm and happiness is lit in the darkness: like the holiday this can come from seemingly prosaic things. It might be golf, chess, rock-climbing, amateur dramatics, hiking, or Wordle – anything at all which brings a degree of respite will help to illuminate this essential separation between your negative feelings and the new adjudicating self you're seeking to build. This way of proceeding is not a mere distraction: it is an assertion of self – an affirmation of life which will, little by little, serve to countermand the gloom. It is also a crucial act of will, which will open up the possibility of your making higher, more functional choices for yourself and the rest of your family system. It is a sort of psychic re-wilding wherein flowers and butterflies and birds are re-introduced into a devastated landscape and some sort of real ecology is re-established. After all, a family is very much an ecosystem under existential threat.

Exercise 6

Draw a timeline of your life. Start with the major events such as birth, school, first love, marriage and all those landmarks that seem to divide lives into stages. Next begin to look a little deeper at how things have come about. Why were you sent to that particular nursery school? Why did you always go on holiday to Fun Coast World in Skegness? How did you meet your spouse? And so on. What influences have determined the direction of your life so far?

Next examine where so-called coincidence has pushed you down one path or another and note any people you may have met that have had a significant impact upon your life. Where did they come from? Who were they and why did they impress you?

See if you can construct a sort of web of occurrence that establishes you in your current context. Then, if you dare, ask yourself these fundamental and difficult questions using that most potent and difficult tool, "Why".

Why am I here at this time in this context on this weird little planet?

Where did I come from?

What created me?

Why am I the way I am?

CHAPTER SEVEN

TOWARDS THE UNEXPECTED

"There have always been Starkadders at Cold Comfort Farm"

Stella Gibbons

"Nasrudin found a weary falcon sitting one day on his windowsill. You poor thing," he said, "however were you allowed to get into this state?"

He clipped the falcon's talons and cut its beak straight, and trimmed its feathers.

"Now you look more like a bird," said Nasrudin.

Case History 7

Here, you might like to write your own case history.

LET'S CALL THE WHOLE THING OFF

What we must do next is practise letting go. We must *practise* because letting go can be difficult and even painful. We have become masters of hanging on, there is no need to practise that dubious skill. What does letting go mean and of what do we need to let go? On the surface, it would seem that we need to practise letting go of the addicted loved one, the dark beloved so to speak.

However, if we then begin to ponder and look inside ourselves, we may begin to recognise that external letting go is but a visible sign of a chain of internal beliefs, ideas, opinions, prejudices, conditionings, inherited views, trans-generational wounds and so forth. In letting go of the outside, we must begin a process of relinquishing all manner of precious internals. This is difficult but most necessary.

It might prove useful to closely examine some specific examples. One that frequently arises in my work with families is the need parents have to feel themselves as loving parents. Here is an example which draws together some threads which we have seen throughout this book.

"Ah Mrs Norman, how nice to see you, how are things progressing?"

"I'm really worried, we haven't heard from Jerome for over a week!"

"I see. Just remind me, how old is Jerome?"

"He's 38."

"Let me ask you Mrs. Norman, How much contact did you have with your parents when you were 38?"

"Well, not that much I suppose, but this is different…"

"How is it different, may I ask?"

"Obviously because of his difficulties. I'm his mother and I want to help all I can."

"Of course you do, but ask yourself this, so far, how has my help really helped?"

"Yes but he's my son, my child and…"

"Let me stop you there. I don't want to sound too harsh or cruel, but he isn't your child – at least not anymore. He is 38. He is his own person in his own right. You have done your job as a parent, as a mother and perhaps now your task is to let him go."

"Yes, I know, but I'm his mother!"

"With the greatest respect, Mrs Norman, your need to hang on is causing you great unnecessary pain and not helping your son in any way."

This could be one of any number of similar conversations.

STEPPING INTO JOY

Powerful negative emotions are nothing more nor less than bad emotional habits – habits that have negative thoughts attached to them. It doesn't stop there either. A negative feeling, with its attendant stream of thoughts or, more correctly, associations will have bodily postures, tones of voice, characteristic gestures and so on accompanying them. Through these unconscious personal manifestations of negativity, the dark of them will spread. So we must let go of them.

But practising letting go involves stepping away. We cannot step away into nothingness – there needs to be a something into which we may step away. This something is joy and wonder. Once we have begun to work on ourselves, separating ourselves from the negative emotions which come with addiction, and begun to make room for joy, we can now begin to centre ourselves more fully around that joy and look for it where we can find it. This reclamation of life cannot wait. There is nothing to be gained by waiting to see how the addict is going to fare. They may get better or they may not. That much is beyond your control and any attempt to own outcomes in that direction will cause all sorts of pain. Un-cancel the holiday. Invite your friends for supper. Be bold enough not to invite the addict for Christmas (they will simply ruin it for everyone else). Go to the theatre, do anything that brings even a small sense of joy back into your world.

"Sit, be still and listen, for you are drunk and we are on the edge of the roof." So said Jalaludin Rumi, the Sufi saint. It is both a beautiful and a funny remark: it contains truth which we must all ponder.

In pondering this, we might begin to imagine a future very different from the one negativity has been busily imagining for us. Negativity thinks it is good at the future. It knows what it will be like, what is going to happen, where it is going to happen and what time it starts. Once the black magician of negativity has us in thrall, we start to make up stories. We invent all sorts of ghastly tales, each with a more dreadful outcome than the last and persuade ourselves that we must "do something now!" to stave off the approaching catastrophe. All negative states are smugglers: they mask themselves as something they are not in order to steal your valuable attention. You surely know someone in whom everything lands on their worry habit.

The wise Mullah Nasruddin says: "You will see two paths. Choose the left one, don't choose the right. That path doesn't exist." Our external world is rich and strange, full of wonder that we have forgotten how to see. As W.B. Yeats put it: "The world is full of magical things waiting for our senses to become sharper." Reminding ourselves of this may help our internal jailers to drift away. It may also be easier to see toxic negativity in others at first, and then begin to recognise these habits in yourself. You might even like to characterise your moods, give them names and perhaps personalities such as Grumpy Steve or Pedantic Barbara. The thing to begin to recognise is that these negative states are your It – and It is not who you are. If we can, little by little, stand in front of these states we can begin to give ourselves a choice as to how we deal with them, whether we collapse into negativity and literally embody it or whether we assert our healthy selves against identifying with the negativity. It is difficult at first, but after a little bit of practise, this process will prove marvellously freeing.

So what do we do? How do we practise letting go? You have likely lived on the brink of insanity wanting to know reasons and solutions in the sadly mistaken belief that if you understand what is happening you will be able to control it. First of all, stop hammering on the door of solutions and outcomes. That door opens from the inside. The first task, the prime directive is to let go of self-blame, self-criticism, and resentment. The situation you find yourself in really isn't your fault, you have likely done everything you possibly could to effect a change, a healing, a metanoia but nothing you have done seems to have had any effect. This is the nature of the beast, and you are not alone. It is time to return to the three Cs but now we can utter them from a new perspective of serenity and healing:

You didn't Cause It.
You can't Control It.
You can't Cure It.

And so we must step out of these patterns. They won't go away of their own accord, but if one can acknowledge their presence while refusing to step into them, they will begin to lose power. Imagine you wake up every morning and dress yourself in the uniform of a convict or prisoner. You don't really ask why, you just somehow feel that this is what you should do. Imagine one morning you wake up and there is the same old accusing uniform but this morning, you decline to put it on even if you feel strongly that you should, ought or must do so. Words such as should, ought, and must are always external: they have no power except that which you choose to give them.

Once we have achieved that, we begin to practise letting go of anxiety – or to give it its real name, fear.

How much of your life is controlled by fear? I would wager that quite a lot of it is – and this is the case for most people. There is fear of what might happen, fear of what others might be thinking, fear of being shamed, fear of financial chaos, and so on. We let fear control so much of our daily lives that fear becomes unconscious. Well, now we need to become conscious of it, and in that process, we will discover that letting go of fear involves us in the same sorts of things as letting go of shame and guilt: in each instance, what we have to do is to recognise these dark things, and then remove them as best we can from our sense of self. This is not the same as suppressing it or putting on a brave face. It is not even having courage. It is quite simply acknowledging the fear and choosing to stand outside of it.

THE BENEFITS OF STANDING IN FRONT OF

At first, this may need to be just at the level of behavioural reactions. "I haven't heard from her since Tuesday, I had better call to make sure they are alright." This reaction is mechanical. It is about you and will feed the fear. Rather than giving in and making that call, try standing in front of that emotion, and quite simply, observing it. Then ask yourself if it represents the self you really want to be.

Or let's say you are in mortal dread of travelling by the underground. It is inconvenient and expensive having to rely upon taxis and buses to get around the city. It could be said that every time you avoid travelling by tube, you feed and affirm your fear. You could choose to begin gently: let's say just a couple of stops on the District Line and work up from there. If you do this, you are beginning to set internal boundaries for yourself.

In the addiction context, some examples of internal boundaries might be: "I won't respond to abusive texts"; or "I won't give in to demands for money"; or "I will refrain from asking them about their drinking or drug use." Once these boundaries have been put in place, it is essential that they are held, and so I recommend starting with ones that you know you can hold. Boundaries are never a threat or a means to get another to change; they are a way of creating a powerful shift in one's own being.

Now this doesn't mean that the addict, and other family members in the system, won't respond in some way to your change – as in the beautiful story of Rumpelstiltskin. They may not actually even be conscious of this change in you, but the dynamic will have shifted regardless. This is because you are no longer uniting yourself with hopeless forces; you have begun to stand in front of those forces, and essentially divided yourself in two between the outer self who is always attaching to negative things, and this new inner self who is observing all that is going on. Your goal is for the latter to over time obtain supremacy over the former: it will take a long time, and it will be difficult. You will suffer reversals which will seem serious at the time, but which, if you keep going, will in time fall away. Your boundaries may seem mundane – a world of not-replied-to texts, and of withheld tenners. But they have a sort of magical charge within them: they can alter the entire architecture of the situation.

HAPPY EVER AFTER

If all this goes well for you, where will it lead? I don't know – and it is not for me to know. It is for you to submit to the process and find out for yourself.

What I will say is that in all of us somewhere – buried deep within the emotional unconscious – is a call urging us to return Home. In my experience, all addiction has its roots in a profound and painful homesickness. There is no word in English for this deep longing, but in the beautiful Welsh language the word *Hiraeth* translates as a longing for a home to which you cannot easily return – a spiritual home or perhaps state of perception that is above the usual drab and mundane view of the world. This call is a constant within human beings: it is rather like a guiding star that one may only see when the sky is clear. To return to the world of Wonder Tales, it calls us to Happy Ever After. It might well be that the hubris of the modern world has layered over this delicate sense in us: it is buried under a heap of mortgages, news headlines, A-Level results, images, fashion, fear of others, and all manner of other "matters of consequence", so much so that to get through this thick crust of ego and false personality is for many impossible. The situation is, in fact, so bad that for many it even presents as undesirable. We have become jelly babies with bank accounts.

Addiction – and this is the case however it manifests in a system – is the call home distorted and even perverted, but it is the call nevertheless. The addict wants a Happy Ever After but is going about it in the wrong way. That fact alone ought to help us in the creation of our boundaries; we need to understand that the addict is looking for what we are looking for, and we have to have faith that they too have a chance of finding it under this new arrangement which we have instituted.

Here then is the nub of this whole book, the real reason for its writing. Addiction in all its many manifestations is a symptom – a symptom carried by some and not by all, of a devastating spiritual malaise, an illness that threatens our entire planet. It is the recurring nightmare of a troubled sleep from which we seem unable to awaken. Yet, paradoxically, that is just what the addiction is – a call to awaken. So long as we defer or deny our hurt, so long as we externalise our pain and send it out into the world and expect the world to heal us, we are lost, it will not be remedied.

But we know how to stop all this. We can cease to run from our own grief, despair, fear, anxiety, anger and shame and be fearless with these hurts. We can pause and ask ourselves who we really are. We can turn away from disaster towards joy, and the curious possibilities of Happy Ever After. As long as we refuse to look at it, the pain will remain. Addiction calls us to hide no more, to run no longer and if we are able to sit with our pain, to embrace it and breathe it into our selves, it will change and then will come the revelation we have been waiting for. The pain was just a shade among shadows, a distortion in the hall of mirrors: it had no lasting basis and it had nothing to do with who we really are, and who we ought to be. It is very beautiful to consider that it is our pain which can reveal to us our love of all life and of one another. We are all encompassed in a mutual night and so, against the surrounding dark, let us light our own individual candles.

Exercise 7

In this final exercise I would like to invite you to think in a new way. The first step in this is to begin to look closely at the basis of your current thinking. For example, you may be thinking "I simply cannot do this!" or "I can't bear it!" If you are willing to accept that these thoughts may be nothing more than mechanical habits, then you can begin to work on them.

The next step is to change the way you think about your past, especially if you have attached a lot of shame, guilt and blame to what may have happened. This is the true meaning of repentance, which really, coming from the French root 'penser' means rethinking.

This is how it ought to go. Bring to mind a time in your past about which you feel shame, or guilt or regret. It might be the time your child was eight years old and you insisted on them going away to boarding school. Or the time you blamed them for your internal state or some time and incident that you find particularly distressing for you.

If you are able to meditate, then do whatever you can do to get into that place. If you don't meditate – or believe you can't – then simply do your best to enter a relaxed state.

Close your eyes and focus on your breathing. Breathe golden light into your solar plexus and as you breathe out imagine exhaling a grey foggy waste.

When you are quite ready, call to mind your chosen time and do your best to recreate it in your mind. See yourself clearly, as you were then. Now bring yourself as you are now into the scene. Watch your previous self for a few moments. See how lost and hurt, or ashamed and frightened you were, and what pressure you were under – and realise that at that time you were doing the very best you could with what you had.

Do your best to extend compassion, understanding and forgiveness to that self. You might like to say something like: "I can see now that you were only trying to do what was best. I see you were lost and confused and had no help or support and I love you for that and I forgive you." Spend some time with that previous self. Talk to them – get to know them and what they were going through. When you are ready, gently say goodbye and let them go. Come back into the here and now. Relax for a while and just breathe.

You can repeat this exercise with any time in your life when guilt, shame and fear were driving your behaviour.

SUGGESTED READING

Cold Comfort Farm
Stella Gibbons

The Little Prince
Antoine de Saint-Exupery

What the Bee Knows
P.L. Travers

Boundaries
Henry Cloud and John Townsend

The Exploits of the Incomparable Mulla Nasrudin
Idries Shah

Psychological Commentaries on the Teachings of Gurdjieff and Ouspensky
Maurice Nicoll

Acknowledging What Is: Conversations with Bert Hellinger
Bert Hellinger, Gabriele Ten Hövel

Homecoming
John Bradshaw.

ACKNOWLEDGEMENTS

I would like to thank the following people in no particular order. Pippa Clarke, who worked so hard in the cause of the family and inspired me to follow. Tim Leighton, for his easy skill as a teacher and mentor. Karla, for her extraordinary wisdom and for opening such important doors for me. Don and Meena for their pioneering spirit. Professor Tolkien for changing my whole world. Jelly the poodle, who taught me how to love. Helen, whose husband I am, for tolerating me and caring for me for so many years.

Printed in Dunstable, United Kingdom

68494887R00087